Praise for, "The Five People Y<

Surviving Katrina"

"Most of us will remember the day Hurricane Katrina tried to erase New Orleans. But only a few were there to witness the fury of the storm and the madness of the aftermath. This is the story of those insane, treacherous and, ultimately, liberating days.

Robert Smallwood stayed. His first-person account, written almost immediately after the storm, is a free-form but amazingly coherent memoir of a catastrophe, condensed into a few desperate and life-altering days.

It is not politically correct. The junkies and pill-poppers, the "black looters" and the crazy drunks that rode out the worst natural disaster in US history are not the charming kooks that usually populate tales of the Big Easy. Nope, they're real all right… warts and all.

Some of the story is nasty. Some of it is poignant. All of it is redemptive.

Read it now and read it fast."

> --*Andy Moore, Publisher, <u>Knowledge Management World</u>*

Robert Smallwood

To my parents, Jack & Olive Smallwood, who instilled the grit it takes to survive almost anything with a positive outlook, and the example of helping others.

This is also for my friends who died this past year: Barber Bancroft, Greg Bell, David Bicha, Henry Hood & Perry St. Raymond. All of them loved New Orleans.

First Edition

Cover photo and interior photos by Robert F. Smallwood

Cover design by Nicolas A. Smallwood

Copies of this book may be ordered at BookSurge.com

ISBN 1-4196-1724-9

I would like to gratefully acknowledge Dean Shapiro for his excellent editing work and diligence in the aftermath of the aftermath.

BOOKSURGE, LLC
5341 Dorchester Road
Suite 16
North Charleston, SC
29418
www.booksurge.com

Printed in the United States of America. First Printings: November 2005

The Five People You Meet in Hell: Surviving Katrina

The <u>Real</u> Story of What Happened in New Orleans

Written by One Who Stuck It Out

By Robert F. Smallwood

Foreword

I wrote this book from my recollection of the unfolding of the catastrophic events that Hurricane Katrina unleashed. I used no tape recorders, video recorders, or notes. There was no time for that. Survival and the survival of others near me were paramount, and I expended my efforts to ensure that. Fortunately, I have been blessed with a better than average memory for recalling details and I used that gift to the best of my abilities here.

As far as the title of the book: yes, it was a veritable hell. Tropical heat, explosions, fire, gunfire, and violent threats. But I, like my neighbors in the French Quarter, kept focused on day-to-day needs and tried to enjoy some humor and each other's company along the way. This book takes you inside our conversations, feelings, decisions, and the life-threatening events that surrounded us.

Of course, I encountered more than five people in the approximate two-week period that is reported here. Many more; and many more of note. But these – Michael, Harry, Larry, Finis, and Arlene are the ones that most uniquely impacted my life during the time leading up to the storm, in its aftermath, and for the years to come.

Preface

Although the nation and the world pities New Orleans and mourns its death-by-media, those whose heart and spirit live there know that what makes the city so unique hasn't been destroyed by the effects of Katrina, but rather, temporarily dispersed. People in Houston, Denver, Atlanta, New York and elsewhere are getting a watered-down dose of New Orleans culture - an inimitable romantic brew of history, music, art, cuisine, corruption, carnality, faith, and freedom. And as these elements return to New Orleans, like moths to a flame, with the focused fervor that tragedy brings to art, it will rise to be even greater than it once was: the most hauntingly distinct and enjoyable place in America and cultural icon for the world.

Part I

Hurricane Katrina & the Aftermath

Life in the French Quarter as Hurricane Katrina Approached, and the Two Weeks Following, Including the Anarchy & Forced Evacuation

Chapter 1

The Calm Before the Storm: Katrina Approaches

I'm lucky to be alive.

Here's why…

For me, it started like any other sweltering August weekend in the French Quarter: perched in the shade of the grand live oak trees at Royal and Orleans streets, sipping a cold can of beer and making small talk with the local artists. It helped them pass the hours between sparse sales and filled my day while we all could savor life in the Quarter; where time is motionless, every motion a timeless caress of history.

We were all there for the same reasons. The charm and tradition of the French Quarter provided the ideal backdrop for dreaming dreams, and for drinking in the natural poetry of days full of art and music that sustained us. This intoxicating lifeblood, like the jasmine smell of sweet olive buds blooming, seduced us and fed our dreams.

A few had dreams as grandiose as changing the world through an artistic zeitgeist like some who had gone before us. Others just lived the dream of sustaining themselves while pursuing their own artistic direction. New Orleans gave that us that chance, and the French Quarter doubled the bet. We reveled in the odds - and the oddities.

Soon, all our lives would be shattered. Or, at the very least, scattered.

And our beloved city, New Orleans, would be changed forever.

The Five People You Meet in Hell: Surviving Katrina

Michael McC

I sat on the curb while Michael McC sketched a pastel scene of the shops down Royal Street. Michael loves architecture and excels at perspective drawings. He's a talented artist, but also a musician and aspiring writer working on his first novel. I'd met him a couple of years earlier and we'd always been sort of on the same page, but we weren't really friends. Then he disappeared for several months. When he came back he said he'd been in Paris and found a new girlfriend with a place just south of there. He loved to recount the taste of wonderful French wines and the beauty of the architecture. He'd gotten by by strumming his guitar and sketching scenes in the streets of Paris, earning just enough from the tourists to feed himself and pay for his rather pronounced drinking habit.

Then Michael disappeared again for a longer stretch. This time he had similar stories but he'd also spent some time in the parish prison, then Brussels and southern France. He'd developed the itch to write. A novel based on his travails was his newest project.

Using the gift of an artistic eye, he'd helped me with the colors for the initial design of the cover I was (crudely) designing for my first novel, *Jackson Squared.* At the time, I'd been working on it a couple of years, and having at least a semblance of a cover helped me visualize its publication. We became better friends when he came to see the reading of my first play, *Brando, Tennessee & Me,* with Nero, a young, aspiring writer. I really appreciated it, since the attendance had been light. After that, Michael would introduce me as, "a playwright, a *real* writer," which seemed to impress most folks while it kind of embarrassed me. I was improving, but I knew I had a long way to go.

The conversations Michael and I had usually centered around art, music, writing, history, and, of course, women. Michael, in his late forties, with few material possessions and a nomadic lifestyle, is a ladies man. It seemed that every few weeks, or sometimes every few days, he was introducing me to a woman and saying, "This is my girlfriend."

Michael's somewhat French habits of drinking regularly and bathing irregularly didn't seem to bother the string of women. With these proclivities, you'd think that he is indeed French, but he's about half Irish and half Native American. The women love his proud, Navaho cheekbones and deep, sharp voice. He's also witty, at least until the booze gets the best of him later in the day.

Little did either of us know that after this particular weekend in late August our fates would become even more intertwined – and then abruptly separated.

It was Sunday, and as we'd done many Sundays, Michael, Rhonda, and I sat around and whiled away the afternoon. Rhonda is an artist, too, and quite successful at selling her work. Sometimes she'll make $1,000 in cash on a weekend.

Rhonda likes girls.

She said she had started with men but had the misfortune of mostly landing those with a miniscule manhood. So she gave up.

I'd taken to calling Rhonda, "My favorite Southshore lesbian." She'd protest, wanting to be the favorite, but Annalisa, living on the other side of Lake Pontchartrain, (the Northshore), had been a good friend for a number of years.

Rhonda was eating Xanax and drinking cool green tea.

"I don't like to take those too much. They make my dick soft," Michael said.

"Yeah, forget that," I said.

"My dick's in a drawer and it's always hard," Rhonda replied dryly.

Michael and I cracked up and he nearly knocked over his easel.

"Now look at that those stupid tourists over there. They're seriously looking at buying one of Barry's pieces. I can't believe it. It's just some squares on a canvas. It's not even art. They're gonna buy some freakin' squares! Now how stupid is that?" Rhonda asked.

"Y'all evacuating?" I asked.

"Not me. I'm broke. I gotta sell something," Michael said.

"It's heading straight for us now," I said. "The mayor says we're supposed to evacuate."

"I *gotta* go. My girlfriend has to take her kid, so we're goin'," Rhonda said. "You?"

"Probably not. I mean, my kid's with his mom this weekend and these buildings have been here for 200 years," I said. "They're not going anywhere, huh?"

"Hey, can you get me a beer?" Michael asked.

"Sure. Steel Reserve?"

"Yeah. I'll catch you when I sell something. I just gave my landlord 300 damn bucks."

"No problem." I got up and headed for the coolness of the A&P grocery on the corner.

Barry, another artist, was on the corner at Pirate's Alley, sitting in his usual spot with his busty girlfriend. "You leaving, Barry?" I asked.

"Naw. Stayin' right here."

"Yeah, I'm on the second floor," I said.

"I'm on the third. And we've got high ceilings," he said.

"Yeah, I might be on the third floor with my neighbor, and if that's not high enough, I guess we'll be on the roof."

"It'll probably miss us anyway."

"Yeah. It always does," I said.

"Yeah, it'll probably miss us. New Orleans is lucky when it comes to that," he said. "We're going to have a big hurricane party at Finis' place. He's got lots of liquor."

The afternoon melted into evening and Michael finally did sell an art piece. It was the yellow one of the rectory doorway around the corner. Royal Street is on the "lake side" (toward Lake Pontchartrain) of the courtyard directly behind St. Louis Cathedral. Orleans Street (which turns into an Avenue soon after it leaves the Quarter) begins there. Two hundred year-old huge live oak trees shade the courtyard, which is surrounded by a cast iron fence. One of Michael's favorite scenes to draw was a night scene of the white marble statue of Jesus, who stands majestically, arms outstretched, casting an elongated shadow on the back of the church. The rectory piece had a lot of detail and Michael had wanted $250 for it. But he ended up settling for $150, since he was in a pinch and the storm was coming.

It's bothersome that well-to-do tourists feel compelled to beat street artists down on price, after visiting the galleries along Royal Street where pieces regularly sell for $5,000, $10,000, even $25,000.

No, it's more than bothersome, it's a shame.

Each time I entered the A&P for refills that afternoon I basked in the coldness of the open cooler aisle for a few extra seconds. I remember thinking, "Damn, it's hot as hell out there."

Michael and I drank our beers and I kidded him about acting like such an ass a couple of weeks earlier when we went to Donna's Bar & Grill to see

Bob French's Tuxedo Brass Band. The bar is across from Michael's new apartment on St. Ann and North Rampart streets. Bob's weekly performance is one of those current New Orleans traditions that, once ended, will be a part of its rich history. I'd been meaning to go for a long time, and I wanted to rub it in since Michael had screwed up the evening by annoying the musicians - and me.

That particular Monday night, my part-time neighbor, Richard, a string bass player, who is my neighbor's (Laura's) boyfriend, played a terrific performance. He had that bass fiddle up on its hind legs and singing to the crowd. The band was swinging, the vocals were great, and Bob's emceeing added the perfect spice. However, Michael had taken to heckling the musicians almost as soon as we ordered our first beer. After that night, I began kidding him about overdoing it on the "firewater," which he sheepishly admitted. Earlier that evening we'd gone to Frenchmen Street, the local music scene just across Esplanade Avenue from the French Quarter, to see what was going on. We'd run into Charmaine Neville, sister of Aaron and the Neville Brothers. She sings a regular gig at Snug Harbor, one of the music clubs there.

I teased her a little, "Hey, Charlemagne."

"It's Charmaine, man," Michael inserted.

"I know, I'm just joking," I replied.

"Hey fellas, I been called everythin'. They used to call me 'Charmin' in school when I was a kid."

"And they all wanted to 'squeeze the Charmin,' I suppose?" I asked.

"Oh, yeah. Oh, yeah," Charmaine replied, sniggering.

"That's funny."

"It is. It is *now*, but I didn't think so at the time."

As fate would have it, only a couple of weeks later, Charmaine would be startled awake with a knife at her throat, as she slept on the roof of a school to escape the floodwaters of Katrina and the oppressive late-August heat. The man raped her, after she begged for her life.

Why do such bad things happen to such good people? I hope they catch the bastard and he's put away for the rest of his days. And then maybe *he'll* get raped.

So, on that night at Donna's, Bob French's regular vocalist was out, so Kermit Ruffins stood in. He sang a couple of songs, including, "Do What You Want To," and some more of his classic local hits from his band, Kermit Ruffins & the Barbeque Swingers. Also, Glen Andrews, (one of the

Andrews brothers music family) who regularly plays trombone and sings in Jackson Square, sang a rendition of, "A Closer Walk with Thee," with such emotion that it would bring tears to anyone's eyes. I thoroughly enjoyed the music and the musicians.

I got the chance to talk with Glen about the influence Tuba Fats had on his music, ("Tuba knew me since I was a baby, man!") and I told Kermit how much I like those songs he's recorded with his young daughters singing and laughing in the background. That's what real New Orleans is about – relating, communicating, sharing, and enjoying life together, while we're here.

New Orleans musicians are like one big extended family, and they all help each other out with grace and magnanimity.

They'll be the ones who will bring the spirit of New Orleans back after Katrina. It'll be the music that brings it alive.

Michael's heckling began with, "Hey, what'd ya do with the money your momma gave ya for voice lessons?" as he turned into his Mr. Hyde.

"Hey, now. It's too early for that shit!" Bob French snapped back. "We don't mind y'all getting drunk while you're here, but don't come in here drunk!"

"Aaaagh!" Michael called out.

"OK, y'all. What do you all want to hear?"

"What It Means to Miss New Orleans!" Mike shouted.

"OK. But only if you'll promise to shut the hell up for the rest of the night!"

So they played the New Orleans classic, and many more. But Michael never let up, even though I was elbowing him in the ribs. (He pissed off Bob French so much that he even mentioned it on his jazz radio show the next morning on WWOZ. He signed off by saying, "And don't come to my gig NO MORE! Ya hear?"). After midnight at Donna's they served free red beans and rice and barbequed chicken buffet-style, so I ate and left.

Harry Anderson

Harry, the magician and actor/comedian who appeared as the judge on the sitcom *Night Court,* in the 1980s, is my neighbor. He lives just around the corner on Chartres Street with his lovely wife, Elizabeth. He's one of the few people who are actually smarter, funnier and taller in real life than on TV. We'd met a few years ago at the old bar, *The Morgue,* (before it closed) after I'd moved to the Quarter.

He and his wife have a novelty and magic shop called *Sideshow* on Chartres Street. In June, he also opened a nightclub, *Oswald's*, a speakeasy-type bar on the corner of Decatur and Esplanade, where he does his magic and comedy act five nights a week. Harry's obsessed with JFK and Oswald.

In his act he has a great line he uses, which deftly captures the timelessness and rebellion of New Orleans, "You know there's a time difference between New Orleans and New York. There, it's... ten after eleven, here it's... 1946!"

Because in New Orleans you can still smoke in bars and restaurants, people still eat fried food and buttery steaks, and they don't worry much about being politically correct. The sheriff got a few DUIs, and not only did he get re-elected, he's now the Attorney General of the State of Louisiana. Sometimes Harry Connick, Jr.'s dad, Harry, Senior, sings and is a guest bartender at Molly's on the Market. He's the former District Attorney.

I like dropping in to the speakeasy bar at Oswald's to have a sweet Maudite (pronounced, "maw-deet," a French Canadian brew) beer, or, an ice cold Pabst Blue Ribbon, which I was weaned on as a teenager in the Midwest.

Harry sometimes hangs out with the demimonde at another of my haunts, Flanagan's Pub on St. Philip Street, a few blocks from our homes. It's an unassuming little place where they run ghost tours from nightly. I'd also seen Nicolas Cage and Lisa Marie Presley (she's cuter in person) there, and had an entertaining conversation with Billy Gibbs from the band ZZ Top. I told him how I always liked their music, to which Billy replied flatly, "Funny. Same three chords for 20 years." He's grounded.

Harry had been quite helpful and generous to me when I asked for help on my novel. He gave me the phone number of Turk Bifkin, who Harry had co-written a book with, and Turk was happy to offer advice.

Harry's a fun guy and he always flashes a smile when you see him on the street, no matter how busy he is. And he loves New Orleans at least as much as me.

One of the funniest things I've ever seen is Harry putting a little black pug dog backwards on his head, with its legs hanging down like thick pork chop sideburns and the curled tail in front like a 1950s greaser hairdo.

"Look!" Harry said, clowning, "it's pug Elvis!" It was hilarious.

I saw Harry that afternoon, the day before Katrina hit, hurriedly moving things upstairs from the first floor Sideshow shop. "Be safe," he said.

"OK, you too," I replied. I paused, since Harry isn't often in a serious mood. I wondered what Harry's plans were for the impending hurricane. "You leaving?" I asked.

"Nope."

After that, I thought that if Harry was serious about Katrina approaching, perhaps I'd better stop hanging out drinking beer with Michael and get prepared too. I couldn't just ignore this thing. I went home, brought my plants in from the balcony and secured the French doors from the outside with concrete blocks. Then I went inside and pushed a 25-pound dumbbell against the inside doors. I switched on the news and watched as Katrina approached. This one was different. It wasn't doing any jogs to the East or West.

It was heading straight for New Orleans.

My net-savvy teenage son had mentioned a few weeks earlier that groceries could be ordered online from Robért (ro-bear) Fresh Market. It was Sunday and I was low on cash but I could charge some food and have it delivered. I got online and there it was: the first order came with free delivery, after that, ten bucks. Perfect. I had bread and some pasta so I made my list: a pound of fresh shrimp, brown eggs, orange juice, Kentwood Spring Water. I added a six-pack of Michelob for good measure. In a few hours, I'd be ready for the hurricane. I could eat the shrimp right away, and the eggs and pasta would last a week. Brilliant.

The hurricane coverage was interrupted with a repeat of a press conference where the mayor called for a mandatory evacuation.

Mandatory? This *was* a different storm.

I called my mother in my small Iowa hometown and she'd been watching the coverage. "You'd better evacuate to the Superdome," she said. "They're telling everyone to go to the Superdome."

"I'm not going there. You don't understand. There'll be 20,000 of the most desperate people in New Orleans there. And if the roof comes off the dome, there'll be pandemonium. I'm safer here."

I assured her I'd be all right and we hung up. Then I dialed my best friend from childhood, Greg Ward. We'd grown up across the street from one another and had been friends since first grade. He's the pragmatist, I'm the dreamer.

"Bob, do you have any sort of floatation device?"

"Not really. Maybe my coffee table? It's made of cypress wood."

"Well, I'm not kidding. That thing is heading straight your way. You'd better prepare. You got an ice chest or something?"

"A small one. It's somewhere. Hey, I'll be all right. It always misses New Orleans. And if it gets that bad, I'll be on the roof. Besides, I'm a pretty strong swimmer. At least I used to be."

"I'm serious, Bob. Since you live right by the river, the water could rise above your roof. They're talking about a 25-foot storm surge. How far up are you?"

"About 12 feet. But the roof might be 25 feet."

"That's still not so good."

"I'll be OK."

"All right."

But I was starting to get a little worried. Katrina was bearing down and was now a Category 5 hurricane – the strongest possible rating.

I checked with my upstairs neighbors, Arlene (she's really quite an astounding woman - more on her later) and her cute, blonde 23 year-old daughter, Jillian. They were staying. Arlene almost bristled when I told her I'd be staying and to let me know if I could do anything. She's very independent and prides herself on being self-reliant.

Next I checked with my downstairs neighbor, Laura, a New Yorker who'd lived through the agony of 9-11. She was staying. Then, across the hall from her, Pat and her younger hard-drinking, pill-popping husband, Richard T., who I'd privately started calling "The Pillhead." He had an endless supply of pain pills, muscle relaxers, and tranquilizers due to some questionable work accident claim and lawsuit he'd filed from falling off a scaffold. In fact, even though I'd seen him run, renovate their apartment, and pick up heavy furniture, he apparently couldn't work. He'd already collected over $200,000 on the thing, and oddly, his "white trash" father had also successfully made a claim for falling from a scaffold too. Maybe the workers' compensation association would like to know. Anyway, they were all staying. If they were staying, why should I worry? I did think it was a little crazy to stay if you lived on the first floor, though. I was sure it would get flooded.

The woman across the hall from me, Liz, sort of the practical, "Martha Stewart" type, had already taken all her plants in and left for Destin, Florida, to wait out the storm. That made sense. But she's sensible.

It was getting windier, and I wanted to see if the river was rising, so I trekked outside and over to the levee by the Mississippi. The river had been real low this summer, due to the Midwestern drought, but it was choppy and had risen maybe five feet already.

I called my older brother in San Diego. He had a hard time hearing me on my cell phone with the wind blowing like it was, so I had to keep turning and changing directions. He said the storm surge from the ocean was pushing the river back upstream, causing the water to rise.

"Dave, there aren't any boats or ships on the river. The paddlewheelers and tugboats are all gone. I wonder where they take them?"

"They've probably gone as far and as fast upriver as they can," he replied. Dave was planning a September 12 trip to New Orleans with his girlfriend, Tammy. "There might not *be* a New Orleans when I get there."

"Oh, don't say *that*," I replied. I really thought things would be pretty much OK. "At least it's not supposed to hit until daylight tomorrow, not at night."

"Yeah, I suppose that's better."

I went back home and continued to putter around while the news progressed on TV. Robért Fresh Market called, and a girl hurriedly informed me, "Sorry, sir, we've stopped deliveries for the day."

"But you're just over on Elysian Fields. It's not even a mile."

"We do all our deliveries from the Lakefront store. We have to close up and evacuate. Sorry, sir."

Damn.

By about 9 PM or so, I was tired from all that and the several beers Michael and I had consumed, and I drifted off to sleep.

Chapter 2

Katrina Hits Full Force

I woke to blaring TV reports at around 2:30 AM, along with the banging, crashing, and whistling of the storm. From outside, a loud, steady, eerie, whistle of winds grew in intensity. I thought maybe it was from the wind blowing through the archway of the French Market building across the street. But after the storm I found out that everyone heard it. It was creepy, like the howling last gasp of a feminine ghost being choked by the devil – and it went on and on and on.

27

I nervously popped between the TV reports and my PC, sending out missives by email. The power hadn't even blinked and I had the air conditioning on full blast. "This really isn't so bad," I thought. But the violent gusts kept punching the dumbbell from the inside French doors several feet in and flinging the doors open, like a spiritual beast trying to take shelter inside. I fought and pushed the doors shut again, securing them tenuously as rainwater rushed in and pooled on the floor. I put a towel down and pushed the doors back once more, but they wouldn't quite latch this time, maybe from the atmospheric pressure or shifting of the building, or perhaps the tenacity of the beastly spirit itself.

A voice inside me secretly asked, "Will this be my last night on this earth? Is this how it will end?"

I prayed and thanked God for a pretty good life. Mine had been better than most, so far. If I had to go, I was ready.

At 6 AM, Hurricane Katrina continued in full force, relentlessly whistling, crashing, and banging but I still had lights, water, and gas. Since the lines for all utilities are under the streets of the French Quarter, I thought they might stay on, making riding the storm out tolerable. That is, so long as I didn't get hit by any flying glass or ceramic tiles from rooftops. By now I was spending most of my time in the back bedroom. The screen in the window had popped out but the open tomb of the courtyard tempered the storm.

I thought I'd better check on my neighbors, so I went up the stairwell and knocked on Arlene's door. The spooky whistle of the hurricane winds was louder than ever and doors and shutters slammed and banged.

"You all OK?"

"Yes, except these shutters keep banging against the air conditioner on the balcony. It's driving us crazy. One of them is already broken apart. I tied them together with a string before the storm, but it didn't hold."

"A string?" I asked.

"Well, yeah."

The wind surged and slapped the shuttered French doors brutally and the sound of glass shattering in the street was nearly constant.

"Let me see what I can do," I said loudly.

I went downstairs, retrieved a 35-pound dumbbell, and returned. I knocked again and this time Jillian answered. "I can put this outside against the door to stop the banging," I said.

"You're going out there in this?" she said, incredulous.

"It's just rain," I said, reassuring her. "I'll be OK." But I wasn't so sure. I didn't know what to expect when I would step out on the balcony.

I opened the doors to the balcony and tiptoed and slid on the slippery wood with the weight in hand. The wind pushed me like an angry demon and thick needles of rain slashed at my skin with sweeping 120 mile-per-hour bursts. I struggled and shut the French door, pushing the dumbbell back to secure it. The slats in the other door were all broken out. I rushed back inside, soaking wet.

"That should hold it."

"Thanks."

"No problem. I'll be downstairs. Let me know if you need anything else."

"OK, thanks."

I went back downstairs and changed out of my wet clothes. Watching the newscast, I thought we'd made it through. The eye of the hurricane was passing by, and it was headed up the Pearl River about 50 miles to the east of New Orleans, near the Mississippi state line.

Then, at 6:25 AM, the place suddenly went dark as death. Everything stopped – no TV, no computer, no air conditioning. The refrigerator shuddered to a halt like it had heaved its last breath.

Still, I thought it wouldn't last long.

I couldn't have been more wrong. The ordeal was just beginning.

The whistling, whipping, banging, and crashing continued for several more hours, gradually easing. Finally, around 10 AM, the rain had stopped and the balmy winds were tolerable enough to venture outside.

It was over.

Chapter 3

Surveying the Damage & "Looting"

Stepping out the front door and onto Madison Street, I had to hopscotch through shards of broken glass and the sharp edges of cracked slate and ceramic roof tiles strewn about. I turned the corner and saw that Café du Monde was intact. Maybe we'd dodged a bullet. Maybe it wasn't so bad.

Continuing on to Jackson Square, I began to see the devastation: some of the largest and most beautiful live oak and magnolia trees downed, like giant fallen soldiers in a battlefield. Walking along the shops below the fortress-like Pontalba building, housing the oldest apartments in the U.S., I noticed dazed pigeons seeking refuge along the doorways. They staggered and didn't even try to avoid me, like they usually will when you get too close. They were soaked and shell-shocked. They seemed unable to fly.

A wide-eyed pit bull wandered through Jackson Square aimlessly dragging a leash. I tried to approach it, but it scurried away when I moved in its direction.

The Presbytere, a 200 year-old museum on the east side of the St. Louis Cathedral, (framed in scaffolding for the reconstruction of the cupola which, ironically, had been torn off in hurricane-force winds decades ago), seemed all right. The building was fine, and the new cupola was still there, but boards and building materials were scattered about.

I headed between the two buildings down Pere Antoine Alley, where I observed the worst destruction yet: the huge live oaks in the two corners of the church courtyard were completely uprooted.

But then I saw Him: the statue of Jesus still stood, glorious and strong, surrounded by downed tree limbs with everything intact but a single index finger.

Thank God, Jesus was still with us. He'd only lost a finger.

The hands on the large clock on the back of the cathedral were frozen at 6:25. Exactly when the power went out that morning. A few Quarter Rats (locals) had ventured out to survey the damage on Royal Street. One pony-tailed man was already pushing bricks that had tumbled to the street into a pile with a flat shovel.

"Where'd they come from?" I asked.

"An old chimney up there just came completely down," he replied as he pointed.

I walked down Orleans toward Bourbon Street, passing my friend Armando's shop, Crescent City Cigars. Shuttered tight. Armando's a great guy, a Puerto Rican from New York City. (He likes to call himself a "New York Rican.") Everything was fine there, and even his new sign was untouched. He and his wife have a young daughter, so I was sure they'd evacuated safely from the suburbs. He'd be glad to know his shop was OK. I'd call him later on his cell phone if I could get through.

Two doors down, on the corner of Bourbon and Orleans is Johnny White's. A dozen customers sat at the bar in the unlit establishment, sipping drinks and loudly exchanging stories.

"I heard the Winn-Dixie by the projects is busted wide open. Someone backed up a truck and loaded up. The cops say you can take what you want, now," a man said.

"Really?"

"Yeah. That's what I heard."

Since I hadn't prepared very well, as far as stocking up on water and food, I turned around and headed back home to get my bicycle and some plastic bags, in case what the bar patron said was true.

I walked past the corner of Chartres from St. Ann and saw Harry Anderson surveying the damage. "Hey, looks like we made it, huh?" I asked.

He smiled and replied, "Looks like it. Looks like it. Thank God."

I rode my trusty beach cruiser (that I'd bought from Billy Ding, piano player and lead singer of the Billy Ding & the Hot Wings band) back through the Quarter, down Orleans to Rampart, trying to avoid the obvious scattered glass and debris. My bike is a single speed with fat tires and a large basket secured on the handlebars. It would turn out to be the best $130 investment I'd ever made, over the course of the next week and a half.

As I crossed Rampart, a block from Donna's Bar & Grill, I wondered if Michael McC was OK. The water was probably getting into his first floor studio apartment.

I passed Mama Rosa's Pizzeria, which had been badly damaged with most of the windows broken, but I didn't know if it was from the storm or from looters. What were they doing, stealing pizza dough?

Rainwater was filling up one side of the street, and then the other, so I weaved my way along until I couldn't avoid it. I had to ride through a couple of feet of water to get to the sidewalk around the First District Police Station, then it was deeper as I crossed the street and into the Winn-Dixie grocery store parking lot. I looked back and saw a group of policemen sitting in truck beds and chairs outside, facing the store and watching the scene in the distance.

I pulled up to the store as black folks poured out, young and old, men and women, loaded with bags and pushing wheeled shelves full of food, water, and soft drinks toward the adjacent Iberville Project. I pretended to lock my bike up outside, since the lock had broken months before.

I slowly entered the darkened store, against the exiting crowd, carefully stepping through the broken glass on the slush-filled floor. The dirty slush was a mixture of water, mud, beer, sodas, and juices from broken bottles. A couple of men passed me, struggling with a full keg of beer, and women were scurrying about filling their bags. "I got chil'ren to feed!" one woman cried. This was August 29, and most people who are on public assistance get their food stamps and cash benefit debit cards reloaded at the beginning of the month. With no power in the city, and rumors of four to six weeks without it, there was a rising sense of panic, even though this was just hours after the storm.

"We ain't gonna have no food for a month!"

"They riotin' at the Superdome!"

"I sure as hell ain't goin' there!"

"Where's the red beans?"

"They all gone!"

"What aisle's the rice on?"

"They got tissue? Any ter-let tissue left?"

"The po-lice said it was OK, so we gotta get what we need. Ain't nothing coming in to this town for a good while."

It was a chaotic scene, but surprisingly people were still mannerly ('scuse me,' 'thank you, darlin') and helping each other with directions to aisles, and also helping to hoist cases of food, or even loaded pallets.

You could call it looting, but nearly all the people were just getting food and something to drink. Don't get me wrong, it wasn't completely earnest, since there was some unnecessary damage to the store when I got there, like the broken glass of cooler doors and tipped over shelves - and all the liquor and cigarettes were gone. The cops had probably taken most of the cigarettes (and meat) anyway, and also, probably all of the gallon-size containers of bottled water. But that was OK, since nothing was coming in to the city for a while. A long while.

I was looking for water, and I finally found an oasis of heavy green bottles of mineral water in one aisle. I loaded up. I had four doubled bags full, maybe fifteen or twenty bottles. They were heavy.

I slipped out the back door, closest to the Lafitte Housing Project (across Claiborne Avenue), to avoid the rush of people coming in. I ran into my neighbors, Pat and Pillhead. Pat nervously watched their bicycles as Pillhead nervously entered the store.

"You can get what you want. The cops said it's OK," I said.

"I know. We're gettin' some wine, dude," Pillhead replied.

"They still have some water in there," I said over my shoulder, lugging the bags back to my bike.

I put a couple of the plastic bags in my basket and hung the others on my handlebars. Then I took off my sandals and put them in the basket too, since I didn't want to completely ruin them in the water. I rode off at a snail's pace through the parking lot, trying to avoid the glass. There was a lot more than usual. It was awkward trying to steer with the heavy glass bottles hanging, clanging together. I got up a head of steam near the low spot full of water at the exit, and plowed through it. The water was getting warmer.

I looked over at the cops when I passed the police station and they didn't even acknowledge my presence. I was still uneasy about carrying out bags of mineral water I hadn't paid for, but kept pedaling through another patch of warm rainwater and into the Quarter. Homefree.

By now the day was heating up and I was sweating pretty hard. I dropped off the water bottles at my place, changed my soaked T-shirt and went back through the Quarter to return to the store for more.

This time I saw light smoke coming from the back of the police station and I could smell meat grilling.

Inside, it was still frenetic. I got more mineral water, but also some dry goods – especially those that were light to carry (so I could haul more) like pasta and beans.

While I pedaled back down Orleans Street, a few neighbors sat out on their doorsteps. When I neared Bourbon Street, Michael McC was sitting on a stoop with an elderly gentleman who he'd briefly introduced me to one Sunday afternoon. That day, the older man was well-dressed, returning from his usual Sunday brunch at the Rib Room at the Royal Orleans Hotel. He looked dapper and genteel, and genuinely happy to speak with Michael.

Larry G. or "Mr. Larry"

Mr. Larry is an interesting man, full of contradictions. He was a merchant seaman for over 40 years and traveled the world. Although he doesn't have a college education, he's one of the most serious, cultured, and refined gentlemen I've ever met. His shotgun apartment on Orleans, just a half block off Bourbon Street, is filled with fine art, books, and artifacts from faraway places. He can discuss the arts and literature for hours.

Then there is the "other" side of this spry 81 year-old – the fun-loving, raunchy sailor side. More on that in a bit.

"You know Mr. Larry, don't you?" Michael McC asked.

"I think we met. You introduced us one day down at Royal and Orleans, I think. How are you, Mr. Larry?"

"Fine, fine. As well as can be expected, in this damn heat."

"Yeah, it's hot."

"What you got there?"

"Food and water. Mineral water. You can get what you want while it lasts over at Winn-Dixie."

"For real?" Michael asked.

"Yeah. It's OK with the cops, too."

"You're kidding," Michael said.

"No, really, man."

"I could use some red wine," Mr. Larry said with a smile.

"I'll try and get you some on the next trip," I said. "I think there's quite a bit of wine left."

"Really?" Michael asked, with keen interest.

"Sure. You should get some. It's sort of wild over there, though."

"I don't have a bike."

"Then walk. That's what everyone else is doing. I've got to go. Everything will be gone soon. See you all."

"Don't forget the wine," Mr. Larry said, with a good-natured grin.

"I'll try not to."

I pushed off the curb, pedaled over to my place and made my drop-off. Again, I changed my sweat-soaked shirt and then left to make another run.

Hurrying out the door and accelerating down the street, I got tripped up on my bike, throwing myself over the handlebars and crashing to the pavement. I picked myself up, but I'd bloodied my knee and shin and probably gotten some bruises. I wasn't worried about the injuries. I had to get water and food.

It was still a madhouse over there, but the undercurrent of helpfulness continued. People were pointing out where to get grocery bags and still giving directions when they could. I helped a couple of teenagers lift an overloaded pallet of food and drinks on a cart. It must have weighed 150 pounds or so – more than each of them.

I loaded up, this time with some canned goods and then went to the wine aisle. I got Mr. Larry three bottles of 2003 Merlot, and then several bottles of white for myself. Might as well. I'm not a big wine drinker, but it was the only alcohol left. It would make do as a sedative.

Mr. Larry was a little surprised and quite grateful when I dropped the wine by. His neighbor across the street, Marla, a stocky lesbian, had been looking after him more than usual and she'd spent the morning shutting the gas off at homes around the neighborhood. Marla asked if I could get her some rice, beans and condensed milk on my next trip.

"I'm certainly not going over there," she said.

"No problem. I'm making another trip. I'll see if they have that left." I made a mental list, then returned home to make another drop.

Pat and Pillhead were drinking wine, and chain-smoking cigarettes as I hauled groceries and wine up the stairs.

"Get US some water, Robert!" Pat demanded.

"That shit's heavy!" I replied, taken aback. Pillhead just stood there, wavering.

"Oh, c'mon. You should be a GOOD neighbor!" Pat demanded. I immediately wondered why she didn't have Pillhead get some for them — what about being a 'good' husband?

"Well, maybe my friend Michael will get some for you, if you loan him your bike."

"OK, sure."

I waited for a moment. Still, Pillhead didn't get the irony. What a lazy piece of shit. They'd been married for less than a year and he couldn't get his ass back on the bike and ride over there? I think he's afraid of African-American people. She's in her mid-fifties; he's in his mid-thirties and without a chivalrous bone in his body. Some people rise when circumstances dictate, others shrink. Pillhead was shrinking. And it was obvious she was just playing him for half of his (suspect) legal settlement. They'd shuttled off to Vegas for a quickie wedding just weeks after they'd met — and 50+ divorcees just don't do that without an agenda, no matter how much booze and pills are involved.

Then there were the incessant arguments and tantrums that I had to listen to from downstairs, and the smoke from "make up sex" that seeped though my wood floors after hours of exhaustive arguing. I thought that at some point one of them was going to kill the other. But she'd basically just whored herself out for a year or so for a cool hundred grand. I guess that's what you do when you don't have any dreams or talent to do things for yourself. You become a whore. And she'll have an easy way out when she learns of the infidelities he bragged to me about. The classless jackass had confided that he'd rented a room at a ritzy hotel for $350 and banged a girl we both know (she's mentioned in this book), with all the details. Yes, in the ass too. All this made me wonder how Pillhead could even get an erection after all the pills he took. Then, one day he offered me 400 doses of Viagra, which answered my question. He was like bloated Elvis now: pills to come down, pills to get up.

Regardless, I pedaled over to Orleans. This time I just went bare-chested, since I was going through T-shirts like Star Jones does M & M's. Michael McC still sat on the stoop with Mr. Larry.

"Michael, I've got a bike lined up that you can borrow. All you have to do is get my white trash-y neighbors a couple of bottles of water and you can use it."

"Cool. Let's go."

I was going to give him a ride on the bike to speed things up. He tried to sit on my bike seat backwards and put his feet on the back wheel bolts, but fell off. So he just walked and I just rode slowly.

We got the bike and I showed Michael how to navigate the easiest route over to the store, through the lowest points of the water. We loaded up on bottled water, food, and a little wine. We returned to my building on Madison and unloaded the life-sustaining loot. Michael gave Pat and Pillhead a few big bottles of Perrier.

Pillhead came upstairs a few minutes later, while I was stocking my shelves. "Do you have some regular water?" he asked. "We don't like this Perrier with lime flavor stuff."

'Beggars can't be choosers,' I thought. Asshole.

"No, that's all they had," I replied. He smirked and went back downstairs.

On the way back to the store, Michael stopped to talk with a middle-aged blonde woman and a couple of old ladies sitting on their front steps at their home near Dauphine Street on Orleans. I waited for a few minutes, then continued on. Soon, all the foodstuffs would be gone and we were hearing that it might be 4-6 weeks before the electricity was restored. We still had running water and gas for the stoves and hot water heaters so far, so things weren't all that bad, but who knew how long that would last?

As I loaded up again at the store, I wondered where Michael was. Surely, he was right behind. Surely, he realized that supplies were limited and we didn't know when we'd be able to get more. But he never showed up. Where was he?

I headed back and stopped by Marla's place. There was no answer, so I left the dry goods and condensed milk on her doorstep. I went across the street and knocked on Mr. Larry's door. He eventually answered.

"Mr. Larry, have you seen Marla?"

"No, she might she taking a nap," he said. "She sleeps a lot."

I went back home, packed things away and took a very refreshing shower. I was beat, and needed to rest. An annoying knock was at my door almost as soon as I poured into my soft loveseat. It was Pillhead, again.

"Dude, where's Pat's bike? Where the fuck is that guy?"

"I don't know. He should be back soon. He wasn't far behind me."

"Pat wants her bike back now. That's how she gets to work." ("Who was going to work anytime soon?" I thought.)

"He's coming. Just chill." I closed the door and went back inside to relax in the loveseat.

Ten more minutes, another menacing knock. "Dude, where the fuck's Pat's bike?"

"I don't know. Maybe he's making some more trips."

"Dude, you said this guy was cool. You gotta get that bike back. Pat's bustin' a nut over it down there. I'm goin' to have to kick his fuckin' ass." I had to laugh inside. Pillhead could barely stand up by now, since it was getting to be late afternoon.

I had to set him straight, "Look, I did you a favor. He did you a favor by getting some water for you. Maybe you should get it for yourself next time. But if he doesn't come back pretty soon, I'll go see where he's at anyway."

"OK, dude. That's cool."

I went back inside to rest.

I didn't really want to get all sweaty again, but about 20 minutes later, I retrieved my bike from the courtyard and tried to retrace the path Michael and I had taken to track him down. As I made my way down Orleans, I heard the restless natives at Johnny White's bar. It was just another hurricane party. Nearing Dauphine Street, I approached the house where I'd last seen Michael talking with several women. He was still there, but the bike was gone.

"Mike! What the hell are you doing? Where's the bike? You have to bring my neighbor's bike back!"

"Oh, uh, it's over at my place."

"What's it doing over there? GO GET IT! You didn't get any more food? What the hell, Mike?"

Michael took me aside, lowered his voice and said seriously, "Look, to get through this thing, we need three things: pinot, pot, and pussy. We've got the wine — I'm working on the last two."

"For crying out loud, go get the goddamned bike."

"OK, OK."

I walked with Michael over to his place to make sure he got the bicycle. Then I returned home. Soon, Pillhead was at my door.

"Dude, where's Pat's fucking bike?"

"The guy is bringing it."

"Dude, I'm gonna kick that guy's ass. If I see him on the street, I'm going to kick his fucking ass."

"Whatever. He's bringing it. I just saw him."

After about a half-hour or so, Michael showed up with the bike and we quietly wheeled it back to the courtyard. He put the lock in the front basket and dug in his pocket for the key.

"Where's the key, Michael?"

He searched frantically.

"I don't know. Shit! Shit! I just had it!"

"Michael, you gotta find the key."

"Just tell them I'll buy them a new lock if I can't find the key."

"How could you lose the key?"

"I don't know. I just had it."

"Jesus Christ, Mike."

"Maybe I left it at my place."

Twenty minutes later, another knock on my door. "Dude, where's the fucking bike?"

"It's in the courtyard."

"Oh, OK. Thanks, bro'."

"Sure."

Maybe fifteen minutes passed, and another knock at my door, "Dude, where's the key? Did the guy give you the key to the lock?"

"He can't find it."

"What?! He can't find it? What the fuck, dude?"

"He said he'll buy you a new lock if he can't find it. He might've left it at his place."

"We gotta have that key, dude!"

"Whatever. He said he'd buy you a new lock if he can't find it."

"I'm pissed! I mean, I'm not pissed at you, but - "

"Maybe you should just go get your own water next time."

Later I learned that they had a spare key, so this was just a manufactured emergency. And no one was going to be going to work anytime soon.

Chapter 4

The Calm After the Storm

As night fell, I heard Michael shouting from the street a few doors down. He was obviously confused about the location of my place, so I went to the balcony and called out. It was still hot as hell. It was still late August in New Orleans.

"Come on up, Michael."

"I've got a couple of cold beers."

"Super." I buzzed the door to let him in.

We finished the bottles of Foster as the darkest night in centuries fell on New Orleans. I could barely see my hand in front of my face. But the saving grace was that perhaps for the first time since the pirate Jean Lafitte smuggled goods and defended America you could see the stars in the sky. Billions and billions of stars twinkling over the French Quarter.

It was beautiful.

Michael and I cracked open a couple of bottles of cool wine – cool from the one ice cube tray I had melting in my freezer – and sat on the balcony to talk. We gulped wine and he smoked cigarettes while we talked and talked.

We decided to venture out and go to my friend Bruce's apartment on St. Louis above Chris Owens' dance club. Bruce, a native New Orleanian and good talker (that's redundant), makes a living as a Tarot reader and Palmist in Jackson Square. I had nicknamed him, "Bruce Almighty," after the Jim Carrey movie, since he claimed to have divine powers. I regularly pass him on my bike and yell, "'Bruce Almighty!'" and he replies, "'Bobby Almighty!'" It's our running joke. The funny thing is that Bruce tells almost all his customers the same fortune when he read their palms and Tarot cards. That puts him in a quandary when three or four sit down at once, eager to know their future. Sometimes, though, I've seen him get things exactly right for a person looking for answers. It's a sort of layman's psychology session. He sends them off with a positive outlook and puts a spring in their step. I've passed many hours chatting with him and petting Trinky, his Psychic Weiner Dog, (Bruce lures dawdlers by saying Trinky practices 'pawmistry'), as he waves potential customers over and tries to make a buck. He's not educated, having never entered high school, but quite cagey and streetwise.

Bruce lives with his girlfriend, Jackie, an absolute stone alcoholic, in a messy studio apartment. They get ridiculously drunk and take turns going to jail for domestic violence. The French Quarter police all know them by first name and the last time they were there, the cops just told them they would take them both in, which settled things for the time being. Most nights, the thundering bass of the disco below shakes the floor of the apartment, which Bruce and Jackie completely ignore.

Bruce always has a bottle of rum or some beers or something.

Michael and I walked up Royal Street, crunching broken glass and rooftop tiles beneath our shoes. The darkness was deafening. The desolation of destruction made it seem like Armageddon, like a movie or something. We could hardly see a thing. Then, the street became illuminated on each side as two lights approached us from behind. A couple of New Orleans policemen pulled up on their Vespa motorbikes.

"Hey! Stop! Where you going?"

"Just up to St. Louis to see a friend."

"You live around here?"

"Yeah, I live on Madison; he lives on St. Ann by Rampart. Hey, why don't they turn the lights on? This isn't that bad here in the Quarter."

"Have you seen this city? It's tore up. Now get to where you're going and stay there."

"Yessir."

"Yessir."

They sputtered off.

When we got to Bruce's place, I threw some pennies up at his second floor window until he appeared.

"Yeah! Who dat?"

"Bobby. It's Bobby, Bruce!" Bruce is about the only person who calls me "Bobby."

"Hey, Bobby. Dat you?" he called out.

"Yeah. I'm down here with a friend."

"Come on up, I'll drop da key."

"I can't see."

A man in the shadows was entering the locked iron gate. "Hey, man. Can you let us in? We're going to see Bruce on the second floor." We couldn't very well see each other's faces.

"Bruce?"

"Yes, Bruce and Jackie, they live on the second floor," I said. The man reluctantly let us in.

We entered the unlit building and felt our way up the stairs to the second floor. It was black as a coalmine down the hallway, so I felt my way along the wall until I saw light coming from Bruce's opened door.

"How do you have lights?"

"It's my lantern that I use when I'm doin' Tarot reading at night. Come in handy, huh?"

"Sure did."

"Y'all c'mon in."

"You got anything to drink?"

"Bobby, all I got is one beer left. I got a Budweiser in there. And dat's mine," Bruce said, rather drunk.

"Oh, Bruce, give them that beer. You've had enough," Jackie said.

"Alright, alright, baby. Y'all want to split it?"

"Yeah, that'd be OK."

We split the beer quickly and Jackie lent us a small flashlight. We left, moving more swiftly this time, down empty Bourbon Street. It seemed that someone would jump out of a doorway any minute. I got a bad feeling, so we decided to turn back and go across on St. Louis Street. We started to pass the Gennifer Flowers (Bill Clinton's dalliance) Kelsto Club, which was actually owned by Al Hirt at one point. Also, Verita Thompson, who was Humphrey Bogart's mistress, had a club there called, "Bogie & Me" for a time (she's back in New Orleans and, at 87, evacuated two days after Katrina).

Finis Shelnutt

The Kelsto Club is run by Gennifer's husband, Finis (roughly pronounced "fine-niss") Shelnutt. Sixty-ish Finis moved here a couple of years ago from Las Vegas and sort of has that typical Vegas look with the sunglasses, permanent sunburn, and usually a gold chain around his neck. He's generally a pretty nice guy (but tough as nails) and fits right in with the crowd in the Quarter. His obvious love for the place has been like a hurried yet comfortable lust, like when soul mates meet. Inside, the club is mostly black and red, with oversized red lip prints all over the walls (I'm not going to make the joke here). Gennifer would sing slow-burning torch songs, Rat Pack classics, and mischievous ditties. This had the effect of prompting people strolling by to curiously poke their heads through the tall, open windows. She's actually pretty good. It's about the priciest bar in town, and I've met many shady politicians, detectives and policemen in there, but I don't know what the connection is. Maybe they just like Gennifer's singing.

Apparently, she and Finis had some sort of falling out, since he'd recently taken her name off the sign outside, so now it's just the Kelsto Club. What's Kelsto? Well, after doing some research, Gennifer named the bar after Mary Kelsto, who had the Club in the 60's and 70's (and went by the name "Panama Hattie").

"Hey, Finis, got any beer?" Michael asked.

"Sure, but you probably won't want to pay what I'm charging for it. What are looking for?"

"Budweiser. Bottle of Bud."

"Five bucks."

"We don't have any cash. Can we pay you later?"

"If you don't have five bucks, it's time for you to go home."

We strode off, and Michael muttered under his breath, "Fucking Finis. He's an asshole. 'If you don't have five bucks, it's time for you to go home,'" he mocked. "Fuck him. Everybody doesn't have money like him. Fucking asshole."

"Oh, well. It *is* only five bucks and he's just running his business, Michael. That's what he always charges."

"Fucker. This is an emergency."

We approached Royal Street grocery, the only light on the street. Robert Buras, the proprietor, was inside with his wife and small child. He had a generator going so the TV was on, as usual. "Hey, Robert. Can we get some beer?" Michael asked.

"I'm closed, man."

"Come, on, Robert. Come on, man," Michael pleaded.

"The cops said I can't sell no more beer."

"How about if ya give it to us? That's not selling. Can I catch ya later on it?" Michael asked.

"I'll tell you what. You got that finger from Jesus? I heard you do."

"That's bad karma, Michael," I added.

"I know who does," Michael replied. "This chick around the corner."

"You get that finger, you give it back and I'll let you get a six-pack."

"Sure, sure. That's a deal. Jesus' finger for a six-pack."

"But you got to pay me when you get the money. All right?"

"Deal."

"OK, OK. Come on in, but make it fast. Hurry up, the cops are around.
And don't let all the cold air outta the cooler. Make your mind up first and
grab what you want - fast."

I grabbed a cool six-pack of Fosters and we left.

"Thanks, Robert."

"Yeah, thanks, Robert. See ya."

We went back to my place, twisted open the beers and gazed into the black,
star-speckled sky. We could've used a full moon that night.

I got my son's radio boombox working and we listened to Spud McConnell
and Garland Robinette on WWL radio while we talked. Both are good-
hearted New Orleans men. Spud's a jovial man and wonderful actor and
has appeared in locally-shot movies, even with Sean Penn. Garland used to
be the news anchor on a local TV station with his former wife, Angela Hill,
before going into public relations. All of New Orleans was collectively
hurting down to our souls and we could only share that misery and mourn
for the city we love. There wasn't any good news at this point, only stories

of people stranded or dying, calling in to beg desperately for help. Many were searching for relatives.

We finished the six-pack and started on some more wine. Our conversation got deeper and more personal. Michael revealed some telling childhood secrets: that his parents abandoned him; that they were artists; that he was adopted by a good family, but never really felt stable or safe. He'd dropped out of the eighth grade and been on his own ever since. He was a journeyman carpenter and had managed to make a living with that between his artistic pursuits.

Now, Michael's continual drinking made more sense. He has a permanent hurt, and alcohol is his medicine.

We finished a few bottles of wine, and it was time for Michael to try to make it back to his place. I loaned him the flashlight Jackie had loaned me, and I dug up a small digital radio out of a junk drawer that he could use. As he turned to leave, I gave him a half hug, and told him I was sorry that all that had happened to him. As he slipped into the darkened hallway, I closed the door, thankful for the (relatively) stable, upbringing I had had. I lived with my parents and siblings in the same Iowa town until I graduated from high school, and I still had friends there. I went to church. I was in sports and Boy Scouts. I had roots. Michael didn't.

Robert Smallwood

I tried to sleep, but wasn't drunk enough. No breeze, no fan, no nothing. The air was heavy and stale and hot as an oven, and the mosquitoes were getting through the torn screens and biting me all night.

I woke around 5 AM to the cannon rattle of gunfire in the early morning. It was still dark and I prayed silently for the sun to rise. I'd heard an occasional gunshot when I lived Uptown, but never in the Quarter. And not like this. These were steady exchanges of machine gun and shotgun blasts. What made it even more unusual is that the French Quarter has the lowest crime rate of any neighborhood in town. That's not only because the police protect it more because it's the crown jewel and supplies tourist dollars, but also because the buildings are close together and neighbors are always looking out their doors and windows, keeping an eye out. You can't see someone looking at you from above when they are peeking through the louvered French doors.

The gunfire fell off as the sky lightened with morning. When it had stopped for a while, around 8 AM, I went to see my neighbor downstairs, Laura, (who commutes to New Jersey to teach college English), who still had a working landline phone. I called my best friend again. Greg urged me to get out of there. I didn't really think it was all that bad, since I felt relatively safe during the day and was holed up and night. But he was watching the drama on cable TV, where they show the worst of the worst. I hadn't even seen a dead body – but I knew people were dying all around me.

The Five People You Meet in Hell: Surviving Katrina

At mid-morning I took a little walk around the corner toward Jackson Square. I ran into Joshua Clark, a local writer and publisher, with his girlfriend. Josh, built like a blonde Greek god, had no shirt on, exposing his tattoos. It reflected the milieu we were in: a raw, rough-and-tumble atmosphere of survival. Josh had edited my play and novel for me and had been involved in the groundwork for the New Orleans Writers Museum project. He's a good guy and quite talented. He said he'd been calling in to NPR and giving live updates, so we exchanged stories. I started telling him some things I'd seen at Winn-Dixie and in the Quarter and he got out his cassette tape recorder to capture it. I asked if he had a weapon and he grinned devilishly while he pulled a large dagger out of his knapsack. All I had was a flimsy steak knife in my front pocket.

A tough-looking unshaven man walked by us with a baseball bat over his shoulder, making me wish I had a camera with me. Josh stopped the guy and we talked with him for a few minutes while Josh kept the tape recorder running. The man said he'd broken into a pharmacy and had bottles of amphetamines with him for sale. He patted the fat pocketful of cash he had while gripping the bat, then offered the speed to us (and we declined). The man said he was moving on and trying to get a room at a hotel down the street, where he had a connection.

Josh was upbeat. He invited me to his birthday party he was having on Saturday. It sounded like fun. That was going to be Michael's 49th birthday too, so I thought we might make it a joint celebration. Josh was trying to line up a place for it and he handed me a business card with his landline on it, which was still working. All the landlines in the Quarter were still working. (And so were the pay phones, until looters started trying to smash them open.)

I walked around the block and returned home, then rode my bike back to Winn-Dixie to get some more food and juices for insurance. Might as well.

Arlene had told me that Walgreen's was open for looting (er, gathering supplies), so after a couple of Winn-Dixie trips, I went to the one a few blocks away, at Decatur Street and Wilkinson Row. The New Orleans police stood guard outside with machine guns and shotguns drawn. One pointed the barrel of his weapon at me as I approached. I stopped my bike and raised my hands in the air.

"Hey, man, I heard you could get supplies from Walgreen's. Can we?"

He lowered his weapon. "Not this one. You can go to the one on Royal and get what you need."

"The new one?"

"Yeah."

"Thanks, guys." I pedaled off.

The scene at the Walgreen's was much less hectic than at Winn-Dixie, but still precarious.

They still had toilet paper! Ah, Fortuna! I couldn't believe my good luck. There was still Gatorade left too. I knew I needed more than just water, I needed electrolytes. A friend of mine, Perry St. Raymond, a lawyer and community activist who was in great physical shape, had just died a couple of months earlier after playing a round of golf in the heat. Apparently, his heart went into arrhythmia since he didn't have high enough levels of electrolytes. He was only 48. We all loved Perry and miss him terribly.

I made another return trip to Walgreen's and picked up things like contact lens solution, protein bars and some cookies. Suddenly, there was panic in the store and people dropped the bags they were filling and fled, running into each other in their haste. Someone screamed that the National Guard was outside and they were going to shoot anyone coming out with anything. I crept to the wall along the exit and saw an all-terrain vehicle full of armed military men, but they just idled by. I got out of there anyway, and didn't go back. I was done with that. Done. I was stocked up. It wasn't worth the risk, now. I went home.

Before I got there, as I rounded the corner of St. Ann and Chartres, I saw two men sitting in the shade by Le Madeleine, the French bakery and restaurant on the lower Quarter side of Jackson Square. They looked like they'd been on a binge for several days. "Hey, we'll trade you some soda for something to eat," one said.

"Here. I don't need any soda." I threw them cookies and protein bars to last them for a couple of days, at least.

"Thanks, brother. Thanks a lot, brother."

"No problem." I pedaled off.

From my balcony, I saw a sporadic parade of disheveled evacuees from the 9th Ward and Bywater areas coming up Decatur Street. All of the people were African-American, poor and some had small children they were toting in grocery carts or small wagons. When those with young children passed I would grab some soft drinks or water, and food, (especially the ready-to-eat protein bars that would be easy to carry) and go out to the street to give it to them. They certainly needed the food more than I did. I had plenty now, and I could probably find more. Most of these people had nothing but the clothes on their backs, or perhaps a garbage bag full of things.

The poor dear children. The empty look on their faces showed that they didn't comprehend what was going on. They were just glad to get a cool lemon soda. The heat and humidity pressed on, like a hot iron on your cheek, but so did the determined fathers and mothers, who stopped only to wipe their brow and take a heavy breath before continuing to trudge along. This was becoming a tragedy. A real tragedy.

Toward evening, I went over to the A&P grocery store to see if there were signs of life. A couple of New Orleans policemen stood guard outside, one burly one, one red-faced sinewy one.

"Hey, y'all. What's going on?"

"Not much."

"What do you hear?"

"Nothin'. We ain't hearin' nothin'. We don't have any communications, they're down. All we know is we're supposed to guard this place – it's our food and water supplies."

"Cool. Well, I live around the corner, if there's anything I can do for ya', I'll do what I can."

"OK. Thanks a lot."

"Yeah, thanks."

"No, thank you. I'm glad you- hey, are those machine guns?" I asked.

"Semi-automatic. They're my personal weapons."

"What?"

"We couldn't get to ours so I drove over to the Westbank and I got my own. We ain't sittin' out here with just revolvers."

I turned around and went back toward my place. As I came down my street Harry Anderson approached with a group of young guys that work at his club, Oswald's. "Hey, I keep seeing this guy!" he said facetiously.

"Hi, Harry. Where you guys going?"

"We're going to check out the flooding to see how far it's gotten."

"It's flooding on Canal."

"Well, that makes sense – flooding on Canal!" he quipped. They continued on. That was the last time I saw Harry during the aftermath. I heard later that he'd gone to Austin, Texas, once things started getting bad. No sense in exposing Elizabeth to all that violence, if she was still there. It was getting dangerous.

Once things had settled down, Harry was one of the first residents to return. A friend told me he held some sort of rally to get people going and get the French Quarter back on its feet.

I rode my bike down Decatur and saw a couple of New Orleans police cars parked in front of Sidney's, a small local grocery and liquor store. A heavy young cop was hammering at the padlock on the door with a sledgehammer while another held a chisel to it. I recognized a man standing next to the store as an employee. I stopped to watch, but said nothing. They ignored me.

After several minutes, they were able to break the lock. One of the policemen said, "OK, guys. Get the water first."

"It's in the cooler. There's more back inside the cooler that I can hand to you through the shelves," the employee said.

"Need some help?" I asked.

"Sure. Just load up here in the back seat of this car, and then this one."

"You want to load up the trunk first?"

"We got the trunks filled with weapons – there's no room."

"Oh, OK."

A couple of bare-chested, middle-aged men stood by with an empty cart.

"And load these guys' cart up too – they got kids and an old lady they're taking care of."

"Sure."

Along with the other citizens and several policemen, we loaded up the cars and cart. Once all the water was nearly all gone, we got them some chips and other snacks too.

"Can I get some stuff?" I asked a cop.

"OK, but hurry up. Just take what you need – no more."

"OK, thanks."

I grabbed a couple of bottles of water and a few small cookie snacks. They closed the store's doors, then locked them with a small padlock they'd found inside that had been for sale.

"You really should use a chain to lock that up. I'm not sure that'll hold," I said.

"Yeah, we should. I'll look for one," the employee said.

A woman happened by on the scene and saw the loaded cart and cars. "Ol' Sidney won't be happy about this!" she said.

"Are you kidding? He'd be the first to say it's OK for the cops to get this stuff – if he could get down here. We just can't get in contact with him. I think he's trapped Uptown."

We all went our separate ways.

I dropped off the water and cookies and returned to Johnny White's. A tall, boyish-looking Asian man with flowing black hair was handing out supplies and patching up the wounded locals as they needed it. Looking closer, I could see he was wearing a blue Emergency Medical Technician shirt. He also wore leather pants, which *had* to be hot in the stifling heat. It also sort of made him look like one of the Village People. His name was Rod, and he lives on Orleans near the bar. He had his compact car full of bottled water, food, and medical supplies. He kept the car parked right in front of the bar during almost all the aftermath to keep an eye on it and offer help to those in need. He became a real hero, humbly helping folks, as the tragedy progressed.

Close by was a woman who looked Latino, perhaps Mexican, who had a habit of smoking cigars almost non-stop. She later enjoyed the attention of the media, and seemed to hang around Rod for the most part.

He sprayed something on my bloody leg and cleaned it up, then bandaged it for me. Maybe now it wouldn't get infected. I thanked him.

Chapter 5

Great Escapes

Ginger and Ray, a late-fiftyish newlywed couple living across the street on Madison, were having a barbeque. They maintain the most impressive array of balcony flowers and greenery on the street, which tourists stop to photograph daily. Since the electrical power still hadn't been restored, and it looked like it might be a while, they decided to grill the meat in their freezer before it went bad.

Like many residents in the Quarter, Ginger and Ray have a joie de vivré and are warm and friendly folks. On Sunday mornings, you'll find Ginger at

Tujague's (say, 'too-jacks') bar, which is a few dozen steps from both of our front doors, sipping a Bloody Mary and reading the paper. Tujague's, established in 1856 and the third oldest eatery in New Orleans, has no stools or chairs at the bar. You have to stand up, but that makes for a more sociable setting. The large framed mirror behind the bar came from France more than a century ago.

We were able to get some ice from Tujague's the day before, when a neighbor came down the street with a key and opened it up. But we were out again. Luckily, Ginger has a friend who runs a bar at 200 Bourbon and she'd made a deal to trade batteries for ice. Even though there was no electricity, the ice machine was still nearly full. So Ginger, Pillhead and I, along with another neighbor, took ice chests, mostly stacked on a light dolly, up Bourbon Street in the scorching heat to make the exchange. It was early afternoon and Pillhead was so loaded that he stumbled and fell twice - once completely on his ass with his legs in the air, then struggled to get to his feet like a big roach that'd been upended - and this was on the way there, when he was rolling an empty ice chest on wheels behind him. Ginger and I were giggling and rolling our eyes about that as he made some lame excuses, trying to blame his falls on the curb or a nonexistent pothole.

"What an idiot," Ginger said. We laughed some more as he flopped around in the hot street.

We got the ice and Ginger left the batteries and even a small flashlight as lagniappe (a Cajun word for a little unexpected something extra). Ginger mentioned that she'd heard that cruise ships were going to be docking at the Julia Street Wharf to take people to Houston, so after we dumped the ice, I pedaled off to check on the news. It would be great to get out in style on a cruise ship. Using the river seemed like a good idea. It was flowing along fine, and many of the roads were impassable. What the hell was FEMA thinking? C'mon 'Brownie,' you could've used your head. Ships, and I don't care if they were naval battleships, cruise lines, paddlewheelers or yachts from upriver, <u>ships</u> should have and could have gotten a lot of people evacuated quickly. Twenty thousand displaced citizens were already down there by the wharves at the Convention Center, parched and baking in the sun, pleading for help. And I'm sure that the good American people upriver in Memphis, St. Louis, and Davenport who are boaters would have done everything they could to pitch in. They proved it later on with their generosity and concern, which was everywhere I went once I evacuated. What makes this country great is the heart of our people. Not the economy, the government, or the weapons of the military.

I entered the Convention Center area to get to the wharf. What I saw was a mass of mostly human misery – people who'd been out of their homes for days, waiting in the heat to be bussed out of town, waiting for help from somewhere, someone. All poor, mostly all African-American. There were naked babies, agonized mothers, and elderly people with pained looks. A woman was dying as those around her tried to revive her with makeshift

77

fans. It was simply too hot outside and too dangerous inside. Most of the people outside had no shade or shelter from the heat. Dozens died or were beaten, raped or killed inside. (Unlike the Superdome, no one was searched for weapons or drugs when they entered the Convention Center.) This certainly wasn't the time for me to think about evacuating. Thousands of others needed to be rescued first. Tens of thousands.

There were just a few bright spots in the sea of sweating humanity, though: some fathers playfully tossing their babies; mothers resting; young girls playing simple games, and boys throwing footballs. The old folks were just plain miserable, though, and trying to hang on.

When I arrived at the wharf, a National Guardsman pointed the bayonet of his rifle at my stomach. I asked him if I could look for the ships. He said that was all right, "It's your wharf," and turned his gun away. I learned later that a National Guardsman had been overpowered by a group, so they were being extra cautious.

No ships in sight.

I returned to the barbeque, which was in progress. The contrast to the folks at the Convention Center couldn't have been starker: we ate well, very well. We ate grilled beef, pork, chicken and baked potatoes. We nibbled on salad and dessert. We drank beer, wine, whiskey, and vodka. We had pleasant conversation, a few laughs and it was rather cool inside. For a while I shared a table on the balcony with Ray while we sipped iced vodka and listened to the news reports on the radio. Laura, Pat, Pillhead, and a couple of gay neighbors were inside with Ginger. We were all talking more than we ever had and getting to know our neighbors better than ever before. This was one of the few good things to come out of the whole series of events that Katrina set in motion.

Tom S. showed up late. He's a tall, articulate, independent businessman with a beautiful golden retriever. I heard that he came from a moneyed family, and that when they learned that he was gay, they tried to cut him out of the family riches, but he won in the litigation anyway. He walks with a confident gait.

Tom lives in a huge, splendid apartment on Madison Street with an expansive courtyard. The writer John Steinbeck was married there in 1945, (when it belonged to local journalist Lyle Saxon), a fact that Tom was quite intrigued with when I told him. I learned of it in my research for the planned New Orleans Writers Museum that I have been working on for several years. It was just coming together when Katrina hit. Thanks to Dean Shapiro, we'd contacted the TV stations and had a press conference scheduled for City Hall on Wednesday, August 31. We were going to announce that Governor Blanco had signed a proclamation declaring September as, "Writers Appreciation Month," in Louisiana (thanks to Gary M. Smith). I'd gotten support letters from poet and NPR commentator Andrei Codrescu, City Councilperson Jackie Clarkson and others.

Writer/historian Doug Brinkley, poet Dave Brinks, Josh Clark and many other writers were supportive. Elena Reeves at Tchop Shop Media created logos for us. Sadly, Elena lost her business and the wonderful *Scat Magazine* as a result of Katrina. I had prominent architect Bob Biery working with us; I'd met with a good attorney, drawn up the articles of incorporation for the nonprofit corporation and gathered the nonprofit forms for the IRS; I had a marketing pro ready to raise money and a real estate pro helping me evaluate buildings in the French Quarter. I'd met with Mayor Ray Nagin, Lieutenant Governor Mitch Landrieu, and cobbled together a proposed Board of Trustees.

But that's all on hold for a while. Now, our local donations will likely dry up for a good while. A little help, Anne Rice and John Grisham? Oprah? Please?

Back to the barbeque.

Before Tom came up the stairs, one of the women commented, "Yeah, apparently he's into getting blowjobs."

"Aren't all guys into blowjobs?" I noted.

We all laughed.

"Yeah, yeah, but from guys. He's into getting sucked off by young guys," they said.

"Oh."

After a pause we all laughed some more. But not in a mean way. You can't really live in the French Quarter and be very judgmental. Most everyone who lives here is little different from the average American, in some way or another. But there is a "live and let live" attitude of tolerance and a genuine love for the French Quarter, its ambiance, history and quirkiness that binds us all together. You can't come in to visit from New York, Baton Rouge or New Iberia and get the same feeling of camaraderie. You have to live here.

Tom came up the steps and stayed just long enough to put in an appearance, but he seemed a little preoccupied and left.

Barry, the artist's, girlfriend showed up in the street and called up for Pillhead. He went downstairs, and within a couple minutes he came running back up asking everyone if they had change for a hundred. He was so excited. Obviously, it seemed he was selling some pills. He couldn't get any of his ill-gotten cash from the ATMs, since none of them were working.

Ginger had three twenties, so he took them with the promise of evening up the transaction at some point.

Soon after, Pat left too. She and Pillhead came back a while later and Pillhead tried to throw Ginger's house keys up to the third floor balcony from the street, but they landed far short on the second floor balcony.

What an idiot.

So Ray and I hung out for an hour on the balcony as he literally tried to fish the keys off the balcony below with fishing line and a trouble hook, to no avail. He even tried it with a magnet. Ginger said he'd become pretty good at grabbing newspapers that fell short, but this was trickier.

Pillhead came back, stumbling gleefully in the street below and calling to us, "Tom's getting out! He's getting a helicopter to come get him! They're going to pick him up in the parking lot by the river. Isn't that cool? It's $1,200 an hour. Cool, huh?"

Soon Tom and his dog came down the street, with Pillhead eagerly helping him with his bags. Subsequently, we learned that the helicopter had trouble landing because of the electrical transmission wires, so, as Pillhead told it, he'd helped guide the chopper to a landing on the levee next to the river. There were starting to be more and more helicopters in the sky, like big, noisy, mechanical insects, and things were getting more unraveled, so it wasn't as though air traffic control was going to guide a pilot in or stop anyone from landing or anything.

Tom is a bright, educated man, but the one mistake he'd probably made was that he left the keys to his spacious, upscale apartment with Pillhead. With a fully stocked liquor cabinet.

Oh well, maybe I could get in on that.

Suddenly, the gay guys decided to make a run for it in their old diesel Mercedes. They only had a quarter tank of gas, so it was dicey. They had room for a couple more so they invited Ray and Ginger, and ran down the steps with their dog to return to the Marigny. The Faubourg Marigny section of New Orleans, adjacent to the Quarter, is the new haven for artists, musicians, writers and the gay community, since movie stars and the nouveau riche have driven real estate prices up in the Quarter. So Ginger quickly packed, while she gave Laura and I instructions and keys (explicitly that "'the idiot'" Pillhead was not to get them under any circumstances). Ginger had a number of pots of tap water filled up on the stove, and some food and a radio/flashlight that she would leave behind. Ray was getting a little buzzed by then and didn't seem eager to leave. But since they'd just been on their honeymoon and off work for two weeks, and the French Quarter businesses they worked at were going to be closed for a while, they decided they were going to have to work temporarily *somewhere*, probably Dallas.

They packed up, filled up go-cups of drinks for the road, and left with wishes for good luck. We all hoped they'd make it.

Pillhead's wife, Pat, was also planning her escape. Her son was flying from L.A. into Houston, renting a car, and trying to drive in. He was going to try to make it in by 10 AM the next day. We'd heard that a route along Highway 90 on the Westbank was still open.

A little later I pedaled over to Johnny White's and there sat Mr. Larry, and, of course, Michael McC. Mr. Larry treated us to a couple of cool Abita Amber beers and we had a few laughs. One guy wanted to see if the jukebox could be rigged up.

"How can you get the jukebox going, with a car battery?"

"You need a DC/AC inverter," Michael said, authoritatively.

Of course, that led to a round of AC/DC ribbing about Michael's sexual orientation. Mr. Larry found that particularly funny, but Michael didn't.

I headed home soon, since there was a new 6 PM curfew. On the way back, a woman stopped me and said that a man had just been beaten up for his bike. I got going and pedaled faster.

That night, I sat out on my balcony and drank wine with Laura and Jillian. We were going through the bottles like water, enjoying probably more conversation than we'd exchanged over the past three years or so, and having a good time. A good time, that is, until Pillhead showed up. Then it was just sort of mediocre. His jokes weren't funny. He put a kind of anti-social damper on the conversation, but he hardly was aware of that.

We ended the evening a little earlier than we might have, just to escape the dullness of his humor, and the uneasiness of his presence.

I can't remember everything about the next day, as the days started running in to each other. But I do remember Pillhead threatening some guys who had gathered by the payphone across the street near Café du Monde. In his paranoia, he thought they were coming to break in. But I'd spoken to one of them the day before, giving him directions by drawing an imaginary map on the wall to show him where the interstates went. He was waiting on a call and trying to get out. I had seen the others too, so I knew they weren't thugs, just ne'er-do-wells. I told Pat and Pillhead that, but Pillhead was still acting like a nutcase.

You have to know when to get your guard up in these situations; otherwise, you'll just exhaust yourself. You won't have the energy when you need it, if real danger arises.

I remember speaking with Laura on the balcony that afternoon, (she had the key to Liz' apartment, across from mine) and we wondered where Jillian was. We hadn't seen her all day. Afterward, we found out she'd spent the day vomiting from the excess of wine the night before, (I can't say I'd never done that at 23). But Arlene wasn't blaming us for it, except to say she thought Jillian was going to die from it. Oh well, Jillian's an adult.

In our conversation, Laura said she'd been thinking of a career change, and with the screw-ups here, and the fact that she'd been through Katrina *and* 9-11, she might go in to emergency management. She knew all the mistakes and the resultant impact firsthand.

"Well, you've certainly got the perfect credentials for it. When they introduce you to speak, you'll have people's attention," I said.

"Yeah. I might just do that. Couldn't screw it up any worse than these morons," she said.

That night I fixed Jillian some spinach pasta with olive salad, since the gas was still on and I could use the stove. We ate on the balcony and had a nice conversation. We called it an early night though, since she was still recovering from the night before, and was to (hopefully) leave in the morning with Pat and Laura, if Pat's son made it in. Funny, Pat was planning on leaving Pillhead behind. Telling?

After another night of wine, gunfire, desperation, and praying for the sun to rise, a white compact car skidded to a stop in front of our building the next morning. It was Pat's son from L.A. He'd made it at about 10:30 AM, almost exactly as planned. As Pat, Laura, and Jillian were readying their things, I asked him about his trip.

"How'd you make it in?"

"I took I-10, then Highway 90, then down Highway 1 along the bayou near Thibodaux, then back up to 90 and across the Greater New Orleans Bridge."

"No one stopped you?"

"They did. They had checkpoints but I just told them I was coming to get my mom – on the Westbank. I never told them I was going to cross the bridge and go into the Quarter."

"Wow."

"Yeah. At the last checkpoint I left with a caravan of ambulances all the way down 90, and then I split off and came over the bridge."

The women had packed their things, having to sacrifice a bag or two to make room. We all said our goodbyes, hugged, and they were off. The car made a screeching U-turn and left as quickly as it had arrived.

We gained a few more supplies, and Laura had left us the keys to her place to use her phone, with the explicit instructions that Pillhead not be let in there, or given the keys. Laura had some candles and dry goods she donated to our cause too.

I got my bicycle out of the courtyard and went over to check on Mr. Larry. He was sitting on his stoop, as usual, but now he was down to his tank top undershirt and he hadn't bothered to shave. Clearly, the situation was starting to wear on him. We chatted a little.

"Do you like pasta, Mr. Larry?"

"Sure, sure. Anything. But I can't cook."

"You were a merchant seaman and you can't cook?"

"I never worked in the galley, you know."

"But you can boil water, certainly, can't you?"

"I suppose."

"I could fix you some."

"OK. Did you eat today, Robert?"

"Yeah, I had a protein bar for breakfast."

"Did you eat any pussy?" The sailor in him was coming out.

"No."

"It won't kill you, you know," he said, matter-of-factly, while grinning.

"I know. But it's not very nutritious. Right now, I need nutrients. Anyway, who wants 3 day-old pussy? It's hot out, and they turned the freaking water off, so no one can take a shower now."

"So maybe it's a little stinkier than usual. You seen Michael?"

"Last I saw him he was with that older blonde woman down the street."

"I think he got too drunk and she kicked his ass out," he said.

"Oh, geez, he was talking all about this bubble bath she was going to give him and everything," I said.

"Those older women can appreciate a younger man."

"But Michael's not that young – he'll be 49 this weekend."

"But he acts young, and he doesn't look his age."

"That's true."

"Well, I guess his charm didn't work this time. He let the liquor get the best of him – again."

We finished our conversation and I went home and returned with some drinking water and pasta for him.

"Robert, you're so kind. I don't know what I'd do without you."

"Oh, don't worry, Mr. Larry, we'll be all right."

"I think when this is all over, I'll have to propose to you," he joked.

"Ha, ha."

We both laughed heartily.

"Where's Marla?" I asked.

"Oh, she's still sleeping. I think she takes something to help her sleep, because that woman sure sleeps a lot. In fact, let's go over to her steps for a while and get out of this hot sun."

"OK."

Larry and I sat and talked some more. He was full of stories from other parts of the world he'd visited.

"Robert, you know some women can be very conniving."

"Don't I know. I was married to one. She made surviving after Katrina look like a picnic, compared to living with her."

"Oh, your son's mother?"

"No, that's another one, though. This was a Brit I married about seven years ago. It was like breaking a mirror - I've had bad luck ever since."

"Maybe she's a witch."

"No doubt to that."

"Oh, things will be better, Robert. You'll see. Life is like that. Up and down. You just have to stick with it, and things will get better."

"I hope so. Certainly not just yet, though, eh?"

"Oh, we'll get through this thing. You'll see. Soon we'll be drinking cold champagne."

"I can't wait."

"You know, Robert, sometimes I have a lot of fun with the women. Like at Sunday brunch over at the hotel on Dauphine Street. I go there sometimes. Me and the widows will get a little tipsy drinking champagne and we dance so much we almost fall into the fountains. We have a grand time. You know, Robert, life is to be enjoyed."

"That's why I live here."

"On the other hand, when I was a seaman, I'd have these women come to me with babies that were maybe six months old. They'd say, 'Larry, look, here's our baby.'"

"Yeah?"

"And I'd think for a minute and I'd tell them, 'Wait a minute, darlin', the last time I was in this port was two years ago!'"

"Oldest trick in the book. My ex- got me to hurry up and propose to her by saying she was pregnant. I figured she was a pretty good catch – she had me fooled – and then, voilá, once the wedding plans were set, about a month before the date, she suddenly said she'd miscarried. Now, looking back, I'm sure it was all just a ploy to 'trick the American.' Her mother, grandmother, and aunts had used the same tactic, with little success. I think they had like seven or so divorces between them. They all ended up alone and with nothing."

"What a bunch of conniving bitches, Robert. Serves them right."

"No shit."

"How'd you get tangled up in that mess?"

"I don't know. Maybe it was just one of those, 'grass is greener' things."

"You have to watch yourself with things like that. Those are serious things: marriage, children."

"She was a real cunt. She grew up in a family of cunts. And they all ended up a bunch of worn out whores with their paper-dry vaginas together in the same house. With nothing. So they'd weave their wicked plans over and over, to try and deceive men. Then they started dying off."

"Jesus, Robert, you're lucky to have gotten out of that."

"Yeah, she went back to London to get her kids after the summer and I FedEx'd the divorced papers. Wham! Done. Then I shipped her shit back."

"That's the way to do it. A clean break."

"A friend of mine who had a long drawn out divorce loves that story. In fact, his name is Larry too."

"Oh?"

"Yeah. He laughs every time he brings up my 'FedEx divorce.'"

"Indeed. You were lucky in that respect. Just get it over with if it's not working and it's not going to."

"Now she's trying the same thing with another guy, I heard. She's had a kid, but the guy isn't stupid enough to marry her. But the poor bastard will be joined at the hip to her for life because of the kid, and it'll be the kid who suffers. She uses her other kids like pawns. She'll do that with this one too."

"That's wicked, Robert. To do that to children."

"Oh, yes, it's wicked. The kids will be fucked up for life."

"What bitches! How'd you ever get involved with her again?"

"Well, she was pretty, at the time, and quite accommodating when I first met her. Cooking, laughing at my jokes, sucking my cock."

"Oh, dear," he said, smiling slyly and covering his mouth, as if to feign embarrassment.

"Maybe I've got too much Midwest farm boy in me. I got duped."

"My goodness, Robert. You know… you know I have a son. He's 49 and lives in France. Poor thing has cancer of the throat so he has to eat out of a tube. When he was a child he had leukemia, but he beat that. And now this!"

"Oh, I'm sorry to hear that."

"When I go to visit them, his wife used to cook wonderful meals for us. But my son has to eat out of that tube, so he couldn't enjoy it. I started telling her not to bother, just to make me a sandwich or something simple. I can't stand that my son can't enjoy a good meal. It tears me up."

"That's terrible, Mr. Larry."

"You know, food is one of the great pleasures in life, Robert. When my housekeeper comes over and cooks a good meal, we'll sit down and eat and I'll tell her, 'Baby, this is marvelous - better than sex - at my age!' And we have a good laugh. Then she'll say something like, 'Well, I don't know what kind of sex you're having!' And we laugh some more. Then I'll ask her, 'Darling, when's the last time you had sex?' And she'll pause and think for a moment and say, 'Why, I can't remember!' So I'll say, 'Well then I was right. If you can't remember, this *is* better than sex!' And we laugh some more. Oh, geez, we enjoy ourselves."

"Maybe that's why you've lived so long."

"Maybe."

Throughout the lighter parts of his story I snickered and completely forgot about the heat, the sweat, the gunfire, and the suffering of all those people at the Superdome and Convention Center.

A neighbor of Larry's from down the street stopped by and talked for a while. He works at LSU and said they were trying to run a "vanilla" payroll run (no overtime, no deductions) so people could get paychecks. No electricity yet, though.

Soon, Marla appeared sleepy-eyed at the door and looking a little less civilized than the previous days. We all looked a little less civilized. She joined us on the stoop.

"Well, what do you guys hear?" she asked.

"Still four to six weeks, they're saying," I said.

"Well, I'm not leaving. This is my home and I'm going to protect it. I can last. My partner is safe in Baton Rouge."

"Why doesn't she come get you?"

"It's dangerous, and I don't want her to. I'll be OK."

We all talked for a while longer until Larry decided he wanted to go check on his neighbor's place that he watches. The man lives mostly in New York City.

"Robert, will you go with me to check on my neighbor's house? It's on St. Peter, by Dauphine, and it's not so safe there these days."

"Sure. What else do I have to do?"

"I'd really appreciate it, Robert."

"Not at all."

Larry found his cane and we left. As we walked, Larry told me his neighbor is a lawyer and he's making good money working in the city.

"But I let him down, Robert. I lost his dog."

"You did?"

"Yes. Oh, my. The morning of the storm he just ran out past me and through the gate and I haven't seen him since. I feel awful about it."

"The dog just got scared. They get scared like that during storms, and this was the storm of storms. Maybe he'll come back. Dogs are pretty good at finding their way home."

"I certainly hope so. I feel just awful. He's about this high, brown and has a spot right here in the middle of his forehead, if you see him. I so wish he'd come back. I feel awful."

"I'll look out for him, but remember, you were doing him a favor, and it couldn't be helped. It's not your fault."

"I suppose."

"I have a friend who likes to say, 'No good deed goes unpunished.' In fact, it's my friend Larry."

"Really?"

"Yes. Maybe you shouldn't volunteer to be so helpful."

"But I still feel terrible. That was such a good dog. I loved it too. I hate to say it, but sometimes I would go over to visit just to see that dog."

"It couldn't be helped. It was an accident."

We entered the locked gate and walked down the narrow brick path between the buildings to what had been a lovely courtyard. Potted plants and lawn furniture were toppled over and scattered about.

"It's a disaster," Mr. Larry said.

"It's not so bad," I said as I tipped the plants upright and straightened the furniture.

"I'm so very glad you're here, Robert. I can't do those kinds of things, on account of my vertigo. I never know when I'll have an attack. That's why I walk with this cane."

"Oh, this is no big deal. He's really got very little damage."

"Let's just sit here for a few minutes in the courtyard and rest a bit. That's enough, now Robert – sit down and relax some with me."

"OK."

A slight breeze blew through. "Oh, my, feel that breeze? Thank heaven for small favors," Mr. Larry said.

After sitting and exchanging some more small talk, we entered the house. It was a nice, historic home, but the putrid smell of spoiled food and stale air greeted us at the door.

"I'll have to clean out that ice box," Mr. Larry said.

"We can do it later."

"OK. Here. Let me show you the upstairs, it's a beautiful place." I followed him up the stairs to the bedroom and bathroom. It was perfectly kept.

"Isn't this nice?' he said.

"Yes, it certainly is. Very nice," I replied. We went back downstairs and he showed me the living and dining rooms, which were well-appointed.

As we started to leave, Mr. Larry said, "Oh, my God! Where's my cane? I brought it with me, didn't I?"

"I'm pretty sure you did. Yes, yes you did."

"Oh, hell, I'll have to go back upstairs and look for it."

"I'll go."

I went back upstairs and found the cane lying across the toilet seat. "Got it! I found it!" I ran downstairs and handed him the cane.

"Thank goodness you're here," he said. "I need my cane to smack you when you get out of line!"

We both smiled and snickered and I walked him back to his apartment.

After a while, I rode my bike down toward the Convention Center and took some pictures of people waiting to be evacuated. One was of an elderly African-American couple and their friend, also a senior, who were leaving, returning to their lower Garden District apartment.

"Why are you going back?" I asked.

"We been at that darn Convention Center for two days and there's no water or food. They say they got buses coming, but they don't come. So we'd be better off at home."

"Sir, if you don't mind my asking, how old are you?"

He stopped, straightened up a little and smiled, "85."

"I sure hope I can live that long."

"Oh, you will. Just take care of yourself and trust in the Lord. He'll take care of you."

A few seconds after I snapped a photo of them, their friend started to collapse. Luckily, a team of EMTs was nearby and they helped her into their van to give her medical assistance.

The elderly (and the very young) suffered most of all in this American tragedy.

That night Pillhead invited me down to his new luxury place, (Tom S.'s) for some cold beers. I'd gotten him a couple of packs of cigarettes from Robert Buras' Royal Street Grocery, since apparently he was afraid to go out. Robert had just handed me the rest of his nearly full pack when I told him they were for a neighbor. He didn't have any to sell since he'd put all the tobacco upstairs after hearing there was a 20-foot wall of water heading to the Quarter, since the 17th Street levee breached. I tried to buy a second pack from a man who had two cartons and he protested, "I'm tired of this fucking begging! Let's go!" But his wife sold a pack for $5 to me behind his back as he stormed off.

So Pillhead and I went to Tom's place and went through almost a case of ice cold Heinekens. Ahh. Tom doesn't drink but keeps the place stocked (for his seductions?). I found a disposable camera Tom had left and started taking pictures, since my digital camera was full already, and with no electricity, there was no way to unload the pictures and clear the memory. I'd replace it when he returned.

I made my way carefully back home at around midnight, full of beer bravado, but still looking out carefully.

I awoke at 4 AM in a puddle of sweat. In the distance, the crackle of gunfire broke the dead of the night. "Someone's life is ending," I thought. "They're killing each other out there." I couldn't wait for daybreak.

I was sweating and pacing the floor in the hallway when at about 4:30 AM a massive explosion in the distance rocked the building. It was worse than the worst ravages of the storm. The building literally shook like there was an earthquake. Then there were more explosions. When they stopped, I went slowly to the balcony and peeked to see if I could make out what it was.

A massive fireball, maybe a hundred yards wide, lit up the night sky over the rooftops. It didn't seem that far away. Then more explosions rocked the building, followed by a continual rattle of maybe 200 rounds of gunfire.

Surely, people were dying.

"What the hell are they doing to my city?" I thought.

I went back inside, closing the French door shutters tight and retreating to the back bedroom facing the courtyard. This was getting serious. It was turning into a kind of hell.

Arlene H.

Arlene is a slender, dark-haired woman in her mid-forties living on the third floor of our building. Arlene is quiet and keeps to herself, but always cordial when we pass each other in the hallways or on the street. She's very independent, a vegan who eats like a bird. She has a sort of hippie spirituality to her and a strong karmic connection. Even with the oppressive summer heat, she rarely uses her air conditioning, which helped her survive the aftermath of Katrina without ever evacuating. She keeps herself neat and stylish, often slinking through the Quarter and peering over dark sunglasses.

Also, she takes her responsibility as Jillian's mom very seriously. I didn't know just how serious of a parent she was until the storm hit. And I wasn't aware of how mentally strong and determined and compassionate she is until the aftermath of Katrina, either. She's lived in our building for more than a decade and she marches to her own tune. She works at Muriel's restaurant around the corner, and the one time I ate there she was very warm and friendly.

Throughout the days following the storm, Arlene stocked up on food, (it didn't take much for her to be "stocked") water, and supplies from the Walgreen's on Royal, and then later by riding her bike to the parking lot next to the Convention Center. Jillian had had enough of her job bartending at the Ritz, and the Creole bartender guy she was seeing had been fired for drinking on the job, (well, *every* bartender drinks on the job in New Orleans, so it maybe he'd been caught overdoing it) so she was moving on and starting a new career in cosmetology at 23.

Arlene, during several discussions with our small group of neighbors after the storm hit, stated several times that her first and only priority was for her daughter's safety. She made sure Jillian got out of there and on to Houston, where she could catch a plane to L.A. to attend a training school. (This made me wonder if my son was OK. I was sure he'd gotten out, but had no communication to know where he was.) Arlene was unconcerned about her own safety. In fact, she said, "I'm not worried. In fact, I think women are stronger than men. We can take this sort of thing better."

I replied, "But Arlene, you could be physically overpowered. You could be raped – or killed."

"I'm just not worried about that."

Arlene was the one who pointed out that Pillhead's behavior was based on fear, and I'm sure she was right. He was paranoid and started dragging a sword he'd found in Tom S.'s apartment up and down the street, and repeatedly mentioned the gun he had while getting drunk and high all day every day.

"He's scared. He doesn't know how to handle this and he's really, really scared. That's why he's so loaded all the time. That's why he's paranoid."

In the evening, I saw Arlene in the courtyard of our building with a new companion. She'd taken in a dog that was running loose – the wary pit bull I'd seen wandering through Jackson Square. It seemed scared but comforted by Arlene. It was a female, so she named it, of course, Katrina. Arlene gave the dog water and started feeding it cashews.

"Arlene, dogs aren't vegans."

"What should I feed her?"

"Meat. Meat, eggs, milk – to put some weight on her. Then just dog food. Just don't feed her fish. It'll make her sick."

Chapter 6

The Calvary (and Media) Starts to Arrive

I rode my trusty bike down to Canal Street and saw the gathering of policemen from outside New Orleans who were starting to arrive. They were mostly from Louisiana outside of New Orleans, around Terrebone and Lafourche parishes (Houma, Thibodaux areas), Rapides Parish, and other parts of south, central, and west Louisiana.

The Five People You Meet in Hell: Surviving Katrina

I was in the Central Business District and saw a raging fire coming out of a boutique hotel. Cops were standing out around the perimeter, maybe 50 yards or so away and I was able to snap a photo of the blaze. Just after that, "'BOOM! BOOM, BA BOOM!'" Several large explosions occurred and everyone started to scatter, with the police yelling, "Clear! Clear!" I made my way down the street where another fire was apparently burning inside the Canal Place mall, from the side where the Saks Fifth Avenue sign is, toward the river. The smoke was yellow-brown and smelled horribly toxic, like it was an electrical fire or something. I watched for a while from the neutral ground (median – the area between the street sides has been called that in New Orleans since the Revolutionary War) where the new streetcar tracks are. I started down Decatur toward my place when I saw a few African-American teenagers slip in to a store window that had been pushed in at Brooks Brothers. One of them was carrying an empty Gucci bag. I couldn't believe they were trying this in broad daylight and within a half-block of the police presence on Canal and outpost at Harrah's Casino. I also don't think the looters knew the other side of the place was on fire. I found a couple of police to let them know what I'd seen and they just shrugged, saying they couldn't do anything about it. I continued on and found a couple more who had 4-wheelers and they rode over to investigate, with guns and flashlights drawn. They entered the building and I went down to the corner by the Starbucks and Pottery Barn exit that had been broken into and watched that makeshift exit, as well the Brooks Brothers one.

After five or ten minutes, the police came out and said it was pitch black inside and they searched the ground floor, then went to the second floor. It was filling with smoke so they got out of there. We talked briefly, and they said they were from Rapides Parish, and that they'd tell the New Orleans cops since this wasn't their main duty here. One officer said, "They'll either die of smoke inhalation or get shot when they try to come out." A New Orleans Police car was just around the corner and they were waiting outside when I left.

But still, I didn't feel confident that they would stay on the lookout, so I rode over to the New Orleans Police makeshift headquarters at the OMNI Royal Orleans, in the heart of the Quarter. As usual, I approached tentatively so as not to alarm the officers. I wasn't wearing a shirt so they could plainly see I wasn't armed. But they were getting real edgy – a few cops had been shot, and shot at, and a couple of them had committed suicide.

I approached a husky cop who had his back to me and tried to get his attention, "Hey. Hey, man…" He whirled around and drew his pistol, aiming it straight at my chest. I put my arms up slowly. The weapon must've been a .45 since it had a huge barrel. I remember staring at the barrel opening while it seemed to expand until it was the size of a cannon. I started trying to explain about the looters, "Hey, man, there's - "

"STOP RIGHT THERE! HOLD IT!"

"I'm just trying to - ..."

"DON'T COME DOWN THIS STREET! GO BACK!"

I turned and wheeled my bike back to the cross street (Royal) with my back to him. Surely he wouldn't shoot me in the back. When I pivoted back around he still had the gun fixed on me. I wasn't really scared, since I knew I wasn't doing anything wrong. But maybe I should have been. No one had ever aimed a gun at my chest like that from close range. And in a month this was one of the rogue policemen arrested for assaulting an AP photographer (on October 9, 2005). This was following the controversial, brutal beating and arrest of the elderly African-American man on Bourbon Street, an atrocity shown on national TV to millions of disbelieving viewers. Obviously, the cop's blood was boiling well before that incident.

"Hey, man, there are some looters over at Canal Place. I just saw them slip into the Brooks Brothers window a few minutes ago..." I pointed in the direction of the store. "Over on South Peters, near Canal."

"Fuck! We can't do nothin' about that!" he said, as he hesitantly holstered his gun. "Don't come down this fuckin' street again."

"OK, OK. Sorry, man." So much for trying to help out. Maybe no good deed *does* go unpunished.

I left and pedaled over to Mr. Larry's. I knocked a few times but he didn't answer. Marla poked her head out from across the street, "He's at Johnny White's," she said.

Mr. Larry was over there having a warm rum and Coke. We talked for a while and he bought me a warm beer. Reporters were starting to come around and he didn't want his picture taken, but I didn't mind. They seemed amazed to find a bar that was open. I suppose they'd never been to New Orleans, which is like Disneyland for Alcoholics.

One of the guys I'd thrown some food to by Le Madeleine was inside the bar. He had his ear split open with a dirty scab on it. "I got mugged for five bucks," he said. He turned around and lifted his shirt and he had two huge kidney bruises and scrapes on each side. "A couple of black dudes."

Also inside was the guy who I'd run in to with the baseball bat, selling amphetamines (speed). He was loopy by now, from the pills and the booze, and the bat was leaning up against the wall in the corner.

I left and walked my bike up Bourbon Street and ran into ABC News correspondent and anchor, David Muir. I'd seen him preparing for a report on Canal Street the day before, and it surprised me that reporters stand there and silently rehearse, then do several takes to get it just right. I guess

I never thought about it, but it made sense. Watching the reporters gave me some bits of news, since there was no electricity to watch a TV.

I used to watch David on the all-night ABC News program and liked him. But before that I always used to watch Elizabeth Vargas to the point of making my girlfriend jealous (then she'd switch over to the *Today Show* and tell me how cute Matt Lauer was). I called out to David, "Hey, David – I'm a fan!"

"Thanks, man."

"But you're not near as cute as Elizabeth Vargas!"

"No one's as cute as Elizabeth Vargas!" he replied. We both chuckled pretty hard.

It was good to have a little humor in the day.

Further up near Canal Street I ran into John Walsh, who does the, "America's Most Wanted," show. I'd seen him in New Orleans last year doing a taping, but I didn't interrupt him. This time, I felt compelled as he approached me, "Hey, John, it's good work you do."

He patted me paternally on the shoulder, as if to offer his condolences for the situation I was enduring and replied, "Thanks, man. Thank you very much." He had true concern in his eyes.

I rode off. Then the situation began to sink in, and I let the breeze dry my tears as I pedaled faster. I really do love New Orleans.

This time when I went to the A&P there were different policemen guarding the front door. One was huge, built like The Rock or some other oversized pro wrestler. The other was a slim guy, with a good demeanor. "Where'd the other guys go?" I asked.

"We rotated locations – so it won't get as boring."

"Oh, OK. Well, I live around the corner, on Madison, and there are still a couple of us left on that street, just so you know."

"All right."

I returned home before the 6 PM curfew. Later on that night, which was Thursday and four days into the ordeal, I was listening to the radio – there was only one station on, WWL, no matter where you went on the dial. I was drinking more of my ill-gotten wine in my place, just sweating it out but glad to get some information from the Mayor and others calling in to Garland Robinette's makeshift show, I felt a certain contentment in knowing the whole world could hear, too. I welled with pride as Mayor Nagin got more outraged and emotional, and stood up for New Orleans.

Robinette asked the mayor what he said to President Bush, and here's what I heard, as I listened in the candlelight:

NAGIN: I told him we had an incredible crisis here and that his flying over in Air Force One does not do it justice. And that I have been all around this city, and I am very frustrated because we are not able to marshal resources and we're outmanned in just about every respect.

You know the reason why the looters got out of control? Because we had most of our resources saving people, thousands of people that were stuck in attics, man, old ladies… you pull off the doggone ventilator vent and you look down there and they're standing in there in water up to their freaking necks.

And they don't have a clue what's going on down here. They flew down here one time two days after the doggone event was over with TV cameras, AP reporters, all kind of goddamn -- excuse my French everybody in America, but I am pissed.

ROBINETTE: Did you say to the president of the United States, "I need the military in here"?

NAGIN: I said, "I need everything."

Now, I will tell you this -- and I give the president some credit on this -- he sent one John Wayne dude down here that can get some stuff done, and his name is General Honore.

And he came off the doggone chopper, and he started cussing and people started moving. And he's getting some stuff done.

They ought to give that guy -- if they don't want to give it to me, give him full authority to get the job done, and we can save some people.

ROBINETTE: What do you need right now to get control of this situation?

NAGIN: I need reinforcements, I need troops, man. I need 500 buses, man. We ain't talking about -- you know, one of the briefings we had, they were talking about getting public school bus drivers to come down here and bus people out here.

I'm like, "You got to be kidding me. This is a national disaster. Get every doggone Greyhound bus line in the country and get their asses moving to New Orleans."

That's -- they're thinking small, man. And this is a major, major, major deal. And I can't emphasize it enough, man. This is crazy.

I've got 15,000 to 20,000 people over at the convention center. It's bursting at the seams. The poor people in Plaquemines Parish… we don't have anything, and we're sharing with our brothers in Plaquemines Parish.

It's awful down here, man.

ROBINETTE: Do you believe that the president is seeing this, holding a news conference on it but can't do anything until (Governor) Kathleen Blanco requested him to do it? And do you know whether or not she has made that request?

NAGIN: I have no idea what they're doing. But I will tell you this: You know, God is looking down on all this, and if they are not doing everything in their power to save people, they are going to pay the price. Because every day that we delay, people are dying and they're dying by the hundreds, I'm willing to bet you.

We're getting reports and calls that are breaking my heart, from people saying, "I've been in my attic. I can't take it anymore. The water is up to my neck. I don't think I can hold out." And that's happening as we speak.

You know what really upsets me, Garland? We told everybody the importance of the 17th Street Canal issue. We said, "Please, please take care of this. We don't care what you do. Figure it out."

ROBINETTE: Who'd you say that to?

NAGIN: Everybody: the governor, Homeland Security, FEMA. You name it, we said it.

And they allowed that pumping station next to Pumping Station 6 to go under water. Our sewerage and water board people… stayed there and endangered their lives.

And what happened when that pumping station went down, the water started flowing again in the city, and it starting getting to levels that probably killed more people.

In addition to that, we had water flowing through the pipes in the city. That's a power station over there.

So there's no water flowing anywhere on the east bank of Orleans Parish. So our critical water supply was destroyed because of lack of action.

ROBINETTE: Why couldn't they drop the 3,000-pound sandbags or the containers that they were talking about earlier? Was it an engineering feat that just couldn't be done?

NAGIN: They said it was some pulleys that they had to manufacture. But, you know, in a state of emergency, man, you are creative, you figure out ways to get stuff done.

Then they told me that they went overnight, and they built 17 concrete structures and they had the pulleys on them and they were going to drop them.

I flew over that thing yesterday, and it's in the same shape that it was after the storm hit. There is nothing happening. And they're feeding the public a line of bull and they're spinning, and people are dying down here.

ROBINETTE: If some of the public called and they're right, that there's a law that the president, that the federal government can't do anything without local or state requests, would you request martial law?

NAGIN: I've already called for martial law in the city of New Orleans. We did that a few days ago.

ROBINETTE: Did the governor do that, too?

NAGIN: I don't know. I don't think so.

But we called for martial law when we realized that the looting was getting out of control. And we redirected all of our police officers back to patrolling the streets. They were dead-tired from saving people, but they worked all night because we thought this thing was going to blow wide open last night. And so we redirected all of our resources, and we hold it under check.

I'm not sure if we can do that another night with the current resources.

And I am telling you right now: they're showing all these reports of people looting and doing all that weird stuff, and they are doing that, but people are desperate and they're trying to find food and water, the majority of them.

Now you got some knuckleheads out there, and they are taking advantage of this lawless -- this situation where, you know, we can't really control it, and they're doing some awful, awful things. But that's a small majority of the people. Most people are looking to try and survive.

And one of the things people -- nobody's talked about this. Drugs flowed in and out of New Orleans and the surrounding metropolitan area so freely it was scary to me, and that's why we were having the escalation in murders. People don't want to talk about this, but I'm going to talk about it.

You have drug addicts that are now walking around this city looking for a fix, and that's the reason why they were breaking in hospitals and drugstores. They're looking for something to take the edge off of their 'jones,' if you will.

And right now, they don't have anything to take the edge off. And they've probably found guns. So what you're seeing is drug-starving crazy addicts, drug addicts, that are wrecking havoc. And we don't have the manpower to adequately deal with it. We can only target certain sections of the city and form a perimeter around them and hope to God that we're not overrun.

ROBINETTE: Well, you and I must be in the minority. Because apparently there's a section of our citizenry out there that thinks because of a law that says the federal government can't come in unless requested by the proper people, that everything that's going on to this point has been done as good as it can possibly be.

NAGIN: Really?

ROBINETTE: I know you don't feel that way.

NAGIN: Well, did the tsunami victims request? Did it go through a formal process to request?

You know, did the Iraqi people request that we go in there? Did they ask us to go in there? What is more important?

And I'll tell you, man, I'm probably going get in a whole bunch of trouble. I'm probably going to get in so much trouble it ain't even funny. You probably won't even want to deal with me after this interview is over.

ROBINETTE: You and I will be in the funny place together.

NAGIN: But we authorized $8 billion to go to Iraq lickety-quick. After 9/11, we gave the president unprecedented powers lickety-quick to take care of New York and other places.

Now, you mean to tell me that a place where most of your oil is coming through, a place that is so unique when you mention New Orleans anywhere around the world, everybody's eyes light up -- you mean to tell me that a place where you probably have thousands of people that have died and thousands more that are dying every day, that we can't figure out a way to authorize the resources that we need? Come on, man.

You know, I'm not one of those drug addicts. I am thinking very clearly.

And I don't know whose problem it is. I don't know whether it's the governor's problem. I don't know whether it's the president's problem, but somebody needs to get their ass on a plane and sit down, the two of them, and figure this out right now.

ROBINETTE: What can we do here?

NAGIN: Keep talking about it.

ROBINETTE: We'll do that. What else can we do?

NAGIN: Organize people to write letters and make calls to their congressmen, to the president, to the governor. Flood their doggone offices with requests to do something. This is ridiculous.

I don't want to see anybody do anymore goddamn press conferences. Put a moratorium on press conferences. Don't do another press conference until the resources are in this city. And then come down to this city and stand with us when there are military trucks and troops that we can't even count.

Don't tell me 40,000 people are coming here. They're not here! It's too doggone late. **Now get off your asses and do something, and let's fix the biggest goddamn crisis in the history of this country!!**

(Ecstatic that someone had finally said it, I ran to the balcony and pumped my fist shouting at the top of my lungs "Yeah! Yes! That's right!" But my voice died in the deaf darkness of the night. There was no one there to hear.)

ROBINETTE: I'll say it right now, you're the only politician that's called and called for arms like this. And if -- whatever it takes, the governor, president -- whatever law precedent it takes, whatever it takes, I bet that the people listening to you are on your side.

NAGIN: Well, I hope so, Garland. I am just -- I'm at the point now where it don't matter. People are dying. They don't have homes. They don't have jobs. The city of New Orleans will never be the same in this time.

(At this point, it was clear that Mayor Nagin and Garland were choking back tears, but I let them flow. The situation in New Orleans was an absolute terrible tragedy, and

no one in the Federal government seemed to care. Poor people with no means were being left to die. We all knew it. We could smell it. Things were desperate.)

ROBINETTE: We're both pretty speechless here.

NAGIN: Yeah, I don't know what to say. I got to go.

ROBINETTE: OK. Keep in touch. Keep in touch.

I was simply overwhelmed, and full of pride.

In another subsequent phone interview, the mayor said a woman had miscarried while she stood in line to evacuate on a bus going to Houston. She wiped herself off and stayed there so she wouldn't lose her place in line.

Desperation...

The next day I saw Michael on Orleans, "Did you hear Nagin last night?" he asked.

"Yeah. That was great."

"Have you seen my sign?"

"No."

"C'mon. I'll show it to you. It's hanging over this girl's balcony on Dauphine."

Michael and I went over to the corner of Dauphine at Orleans, and there hung a large, handmade sign on a white sheet, flapping in the slight breeze:

NAGIN for PRESIDENT

"That's great. That's awesome, Michael." We shook hands earnestly.

"Yeah, it was about time someone said something."

"No shit."

I rode back toward Johnny White's.

On Orleans near Bourbon, a man slowly pedaled along with a basket on his bicycle, filled with something wrapped in white butchers' paper. "You want some deer sausage? Anyone want some deer sausage?" he said. "It's been on dry ice and it's still good."

"Where'd you get it?" I asked.

"From Lucky Dogs. It was in the freezer and on dry ice. It was the owner's personal stock, and he wanted me to see if I could give it away to someone who'd cook it up."

Thinking of Ginger and Ray's propane grill, I thought I could cook it and hand it out. I inspected the package and it was still cool, and it looked and smelled fine, so I accepted the venison. There must've been 30 pounds or so. I rushed back to Madison Street and fired up the grill. It was hot as Hades grilling in the afternoon sun. But within 20 minutes, I had a couple of aluminum foil covered containers full of the freshly-grilled game, and I put some more on the grill, turned it down low and headed over to the A&P to see if the police wanted some. They were the first priority.

A couple of cops were sitting in a car across from Royal Street Grocery, with the officer in the driver's side on the phone and his partner dozing off, so I offered it to them. They both hungrily took some. At A&P, though, the policemen were more suspicious of the meat since it was maybe five days into the aftermath of Katina. Then I told them about Pillhead dragging the sword up and down the street and how he was scaring Arlene.

"Well, if he comes up this way with it, we'll light his ass up!"

"Good."

"And you know what'll happen to us?"

"Nothing?"

"Not a damn thing," he said, and they both laughed while I joined in.

I continued on, going the long way around the block, (to avoid the vultures at Johnny White's bar), to get to Mr. Larry's, where he was sitting and talking with Marla. They both got several of the warm links and thanked me profusely. There were a few sailor-like jokes about me giving them some "'hot sausage.'" Then I went over to Johnny White's Bar, and the crowd snapped the rest up, lavishing me with great thanks.

I returned and grilled up the rest of it, eating some myself, and giving the rest to Katrina, our new watchdog on Madison Street.

Chapter 7

Making the Best of It

It was Saturday, and I continued to make my runs to the Convention Center parking lot for provisions. I passed a man on a bicycle and we spoke. "There's still food and water in the Convention Center parking lot."

"I'm just going to check on the mules in the stables under the bridge. The ones in other stables aren't in such good shape. Some are standing in water, because the fools didn't get them outta there."

"You a carriage driver?"

"Yeah. Maybe I'll get one out to stretch his legs, if I can get to everything to hook him up."

"That'd be cool," I said. The carriages were one of the things that make the French Quarter what it is. It adds to the romance and charm of the place.

Later, Mr. Larry and I were hanging out at Johnny White's. The throng of media was growing, coming from all over: Australia, Canada, Great Britain, Austria, Sweden, Japan. Their continual hounding aggravated Mr. Larry, but most folks didn't mind. Joe, the bartender who'd simply volunteered when the bar was short-handed, was eating it up.

The mule driver I'd seen when riding my bike on Decatur pulled up with an empty carriage to a lively reception. "Anybody want to take a ride?" he asked.

"C'mon Mr. Larry, let's go. It'll be fun," I said.

"Why, in all my 40 years here, do you know I've never taken a ride in one of those things?" Mr. Larry said.

"Neither have I. C'mon, let's go, it'll be fun!" So Mr. Larry slipped out of the bar stool with his drink in one hand and cane in the other. I helped him up into the red leather seat. Soon the carriage was full, and off we went with cheers from the bar and cameras clicking.

As we passed a policeman he said, "Good. Go ahead; you might as well cheer folks up a little!"

I was surprised at how smooth the ride was: we accelerated steadily and you could feel the solid equine strength pulling us along. I looked over at Mr. Larry and his face was covered with delight.

"It *is* fun! I'm glad we're taking this ride, Robert," Mr. Larry said.

We wove through the traffic-less French Quarter laughing and cheering, elated at our little ride. We went almost to Esplanade, then came up Decatur Street and stopped at Molly's on the Market for a refill. Jim Monaghan's son runs it now and he'd been opening the place for a few hours each day, after a few days of struggling to get the place back in shape and get someone to work.

Writer and poet Andrei Codrescu was standing outside drinking with poet Dave Brinks. I got out of the carriage and gave Andrei a big hug, then Dave. It was good to see them. We'd survived for almost a week. Dave has a wonderful talent and Andrei is a friend and mentor to him. Dave runs the regular, "17 Poets" readings on Thursdays at the dank Goldmine Saloon on Dauphine. In the spring and fall he hosts the, *Festival of the*

Imagination, which includes poetry, spoken word, dance, visual art, and other art forms. The Goldmine used to be horse stables, and six nights a week it's not a poetry kind of place, but Dave has kept the words alive by providing a platform for not only local poets, but outstanding ones from New York, California – all over. I'd read a couple of my poems there, like the one I wrote for Tuba Fats when he died, and also another one, which didn't go over so well, "'My Penis is a Weapon of Mass Destruction.'" You could've heard a roach crawl across the floor. My friend Armando thought it was very funny, but Dave might as well have had a hook with him as fast as he shooed me off the stage! It was awkwardly funny. I felt like an idiot. A perverse idiot. How come everyone is riveted and laughs when Andrei reads poems about sex and pussy? I guess I haven't reached that status yet. Oh well. I'd also done a reading of a scene of my play there, *Brando, Tennessee & Me,* with Josh Clark, who'd helped edit it for me. That did go over pretty well. People actually laughed at lines that were supposed to be humorous. Mostly, though, I love going to the Goldmine and just listening. It puts things in perspective and time freezes sweetly while you're there.

When Andrei reads some of his stuff there it's usually to a packed house. In fact, that's where I first met him – I approached him after a reading and told him about my New Orleans Writers Museum project. He's been very supportive. Since then I've had the pleasure of conversing or joking with him over coffee at CC's or drinks at Molly's or the Goldmine. He's a kick.

He's also an amazing man. He grew up in Romania, fled the persecution of Jews there, and ended up in New York hanging out with beat poets like Allen Ginsberg in the 1960s. Andrei's poetry is beautiful and it complements the English language, even though he didn't really learn English until he was in his 20s.

But I'm not going to put my nose up his ass. I like his writing and his sense of humor but I don't agree with everything he says. I totally disagree with the contention he made in the *New York Times* in September 2005 that New Orleans was never going to come back; that it had been destroyed, and that the artists, musicians, and poets would move on. I couldn't disagree more. These people will fuel one of the greatest artistic movements ever. I believe that all the new paintings, sculptures, photographs, poems, plays, music - and even cuisine that are created as a result of the tragedy of Katrina will form an identifiable zeitgeist of artistic expression. If your spiritual home is New Orleans, you can never really leave it, even if you're temporarily living somewhere else. Right now, I'm dreaming of Fiorella's fried oyster po-boys; cold Miller High Life and marinated crab claws at Coop's; hanging out listening to music at the Apple Barrel on Frenchmen Street, maybe smoking a cigar with Coco Robichaux between sets; strolling by the river or writing poetry in Jackson Square. The buildings of the French Quarter are still there, the memories and history are still there and when the people return, the art, poetry and romance will be back again and more cogent than ever.

After we got fresh drinks and loaded back up, we pulled out and went up Decatur to St. Peter, where a different New Orleans cop stopped the carriage, saying that we were endangering their security operations with our fun. We had to get out, and Mr. Larry was ready to go anyway, since the media were shoving their cameras in our faces. When we got back to Johnny White's, Michael came down the street with a small grocery cart full of his possessions. He looked like a mad dog. He was acting just plain crazy.

"Where's the hell's my fire extinguishers? I want my fire extinguishers!"

"OK, OK, Mike. I'll go get them. Where are they?"

"Inside the bar! They won't let me back in!"

"No wonder," Mr. Larry whispered.

I went into Johnny White's and found the fire extinguishers in the corner, and brought them outside to him. He still didn't seem satisfied. I wondered why he even needed them if he wasn't going to stay in his apartment anymore.

Michael had gone mad, lost his mind.

He'd told me a couple of days earlier about the shooting all night outside his apartment. Remember, he lives close to the Iberville Projects, but he'd been joking about it. He said he was like "'ricochet rabbit'" hiding in different corners of the apartment upstairs that he'd broken into, to try and avoid the bullets. But apparently it had a delayed effect, and got the best of him. He'd snapped. Post traumatic stress or something.

We didn't see Michael any more after that. I hope he's OK and he regains his senses.

Chapter 8

Lock Down

The next day I went over to Ginger and Ray's apartment to use their propane gas grill to heat up some water. Our gas had been turned off, and Mr. Larry and I were really hankering for a cup of hot coffee in the morning. Once I got the pot near boiling, I scurried down the three flights of steps, put the pot in my bike basket and rode to Orleans and past Bourbon with a jar of instant coffee. I knocked on Mr. Larry's door and he soon answered. "Ready for some hot coffee, Mr. Larry?"

"How?"

"I've got some instant Community Coffee, and I heated up some water on my neighbor's grill."

"Oh, my, yes. Thank you so much, Robert."

He retrieved a couple of coffee cups and we sat, sipped our coffee and chatted while the morning heated up.

"You know, Robert, when this is all over, I think I'll have to propose to you," he said with an impish grin.

"Very funny. OK, then, you're going to be the woman."

We both laughed.

After coffee I rode over toward the Convention Center to get some MREs and water. There were pallets of the supplies there.

The city was now filling with National Guardsmen, County Sheriffs from all over the nation – I saw Arizona, South Carolina, Georgia, Indiana, Ohio, Michigan and New York plates – and any and all other kinds of law enforcement officers, including DEA, ATF, INS and the FBI. I was never so glad to see the law in my life. I felt proud and increasingly more patriotic and secure.

At the Convention Center parking lot, since someone had taken a case of water and was selling them to the thirsting crowd, we were only allowed to get one bottle and one MRE. When I was in waiting in line, I took a few minutes to talk with the National Guardsmen. "Where y'all from?"

"Arkansas."

"Were y'all in Iraq?"

"Yeah. Just got back. This was supposed to be our vacation."

"Are those semi-automatic rifles?"

"Yeah. But we also brought our own weapons – we told the Sarge – since they only gave us five rounds. I hope we see some looters. I want to kill somebody."

"Why weren't y'all here earlier? We could've used you being here a few days ago when it was out of control."

"You don't understand. It takes a while to deploy. First we gotta get our orders, then we gotta get our weapons and ammo issued – it just don't happen overnight."

"Huh. Well, we sure appreciate y'all being here. I don't know what we'd have done without you."

"Not a problem. Glad to help."

"Thanks again, guys."

I toured around the Central Business District and then back to Mr. Larry's to drop off the MRE and water. Mr. Larry wanted to go back to check on his friend's house again, and to clear out the fridge. "Robert, won't you go with me, again?"

"Sure, I'll go."

"I really appreciate it. I don't know what I'd do without you."

"Oh, don't worry about it, Mr. Larry."

We walked around the block and entered the house to a much greater stench than before. It smacked me in the face when I opened the door to the refrigerator. I just plugged my nose and emptied it out into a trash bag and then propped the door open. We locked up and I lugged the bag out to the street.

"Thank you so much, Robert."

"No problem."

"Let's go for a drink at Johnny White's. Want to?"

"Sure. You don't have to buy me a drink though."

"Oh, don't say that. I'd like to offer you a drink. It's on me. Please accept it. You've been so kind. I'd be offended if you didn't accept."

"All right, then."

We had a couple of drinks at the bar, then retired to the stoop across the street, to get out of the sun.

Mary, Terry, and a thuggish drug dealer were over there sipping on bottles of liquor. A drunk, gay, African-American guy approached me and said that he hoped I wouldn't be offended, but that I was, "real hot." I didn't see how he could be thinking along those lines at this point. It was getting loud and raucous, and most of the group was out of control. They'd been drinking all day... well... they'd been drinking all week. Mary, who is homeless and got that way most days anyway, was really getting out of control. Spittle was coming though her picket-fence teeth.

Mr. Larry was getting perturbed with the loudness. Then, a man came close to him with a camera, and he told him, "Please don't snap my picture," but the man did it anyway. Mr. Larry was livid and started yelling at the man. I stepped in front of him, "Don't you have any respect? The man said he didn't want his picture taken. GET THE FUCK OUT OF HERE!" I yelled.

"Fuck you."

"FUCK YOU! I SAID GET THE FUCK OUT OF HERE!"

The man pulled his hand out from behind his back and pointed his index finger at me with his thumb cocked back, as if he had a gun. He cocked the imaginary trigger and mimicked a shooting motion.

"I'll remember you. Don't worry, you'll get it!" he said.

"Oh, really? If you've got a gun, where is it? Do you need a gun, you coward?" I asked.

"I'll remember you," he said, continuing his shooting motion, aimed at my chest.

Just to be safe(r), I didn't approach him, but I stood my ground. "You got a gun? Why don't you show it to the cops, big man? Go ahead, show the cops your gun!" I said.

But there were no cops in sight.

A smaller man jumped in front of me, "That's my neighbor. He's OK. But I've never seen him act like this. He's losing his mind!"

"Well, tell him to get the fuck out of here before I knock his fucking teeth out and shut him up."

The man ran over to his neighbor and pleaded with him to go back up the street and go inside. He stayed and continued his taunting act.

Then a police car came down the street. The feigning shooter stopped them and gave them his story. Then they came down to where I was, standing in front of Mr. Larry. "He's got a gun," I said. He's been using his hand, threatening me like he's got a gun."

"There's three sides to every story, man. Your side, his side, and the truth.

"No, really, I'm telling you the truth."

Mr. Larry nudged me out of the way with his cane and went to the police car window and explained calmly what had happened. The police backed up and had the faux shooter put his arms behind his head as they searched him.

He didn't have a gun.

We decided to leave. It was out of hand and getting a little dangerous. I walked Mr. Larry home and on the way back I ran into Finis.

"I'm gonna go with Chris Owens and her husband. I can take a lot of shit, but not these damn mosquitoes. I don't want to get West Nile or something. I knew a guy who was big and muscular and he got that shit, and he fucking crippled now. Nothing left of him," Finis said.

"Yeah, that's not something to fuck around with, really. Maybe I should go too."

As it ended up, Finis stayed anyway, through the whole thing.

After seeing him, though, I went by the A&P, remembering again that mosquitoes had bitten me up the night before. The same two policemen were there, only now their heads hung down with fatigue.

"Hey, can I get some bug spray?"

"Sure."

After seeing a guy get thrown out a few days earlier for filling a bag full of stuff, (when he was only supposed to be getting cat food), I just went in with my open hands. I carefully stepped through the shattered glass door on my toes. Inside the darkened and foul-smelling building, I found three cans of Raid. When I came out, I showed the cans to them and the over-muscled cop looked agitated. "Dude, do me a favor. Put two of those back."

(For those of you who thought all the New Orleans cops were looting, take note of how closely he was watching the place.)

"But one's for the old man around the corner I'm looking out for and another's for my neighbor. She's still in my building."

"All right then."

I back went over to Mr. Larry's and offered him some bug spray, but he didn't want any. It was getting to be six o'clock, so I went home. Arlene didn't want any either, so I sprayed the heck out of my place and tried to pull the broken screen most of the way closed.

Chapter 9

A Little Parade

Labor Day had arrived. But instead of the planned debauchery for the "Southern Decadence" celebration, a mostly gay annual event, the streets were quiet. But that didn't dampen the spirits of a handful of locals who were determined to have a little fun and are always looking for an excuse for a parade.

It started with a couple of young women dressed scantily, twirling parasols, and walking tiny dressed-up dogs. They started doing a little second line jig in front of Johnny White's. "C'mon y'all! We're gonna have a parade at one o'clock! Go get dressed up! C'mon y'all! It's Decadence weekend!"

Then a long-haired, shirtless man appeared in short cutoff jean shorts, a hat and sunglasses holding a sign, "Life Goes On?" The media was starting to assemble. Here was another story of the insanity of the French Quarter. *How could they possibly think of having a parade when there is no food or water?*

Because it's New Orleans, baby.

"C'mon y'all," the girls called out, stirring up the customers at Johnny White's.

Thinking I might as well do my part to cheer people (and myself) up, I went home, took my shirt off, then put on a few strands of Mardi Gras beads and my waterproof, navy blue fedora. Why not?

When I returned the media were really swarming. They loved this. Next thing I knew, BBC News was taking pictures and interviews were flying. (Afterward, I found the pic of me on the BBC News website). About eight or ten people joined the little procession. We danced in the street and then took off and held our makeshift little parade.

It was *so* New Orleans.

That night, I spoke with my mother and found out that my son was on his way to my sister's house in Georgia. He would enroll in Brookwood High School the next day.

Thank God.

Chapter 10

I Evacuate

I decided it was time to go. Things weren't getting better and there was no end in sight. I'd found my son and he was enrolling in a new high school. The mayor had issued a more serious "mandatory evacuation," and the city was filled with heavily armed police, S.W.A.T. teams, military police, and the 82nd Airborne Division. The stench was growing and the flies were getting bigger by the day.

The water was back on, but it wasn't certifiably clean yet. So I took a shower, being careful not to splash my face with the still-contaminated water, then used drinking water to wash my face and shave. I changed into fresh clothes and packed up. Yes, it was time to go.

Michael had lost his mind and scattered. Larry was determined not to leave. Harry Anderson was in Austin. Finis was sticking it out and doing daily interviews for the media (soon he'd be feeding 3,000 people a day), and Arlene had Katrina the pit bull to protect her.

I went to say goodbye to Mr. Larry. When I arrived, he was calmly sitting on his stoop and reading *The Man Who Killed Rasputin*. "So, you're leaving, Robert?"

"Yes. Gotta go take care of my kid."

"I can understand that. Well, when you come back, we'll have to share a glass of cold champagne."

"Sounds good. Goodbye, Mr. Larry. And take care of yourself." I gave him a hug.

"I'll be fine," he said.

Arlene generously offered to walk with me and ride my bike back, but I didn't want to be a bother and I thought I could hitch a ride with someone. I gave her a hug, feeling the bones sticking out of her ribcage, and I think she held on just a little. We'd made it, made it that far; we knew each other better and had gained a mutual respect. But it was time to say goodbye.

I lugged my bags down Decatur with my thumb out. Police and news vehicles passed, not slowing. One foreign news team was taking pictures of Jackson Square, so I asked them for a ride. "No, we cannot," a reported replied with a thick accent. *How could they refuse? They had gleaned scenes for their audiences, couldn't they help – just a little?*

At Wilkinson Row, just across from Walgreen's, a car quickly pulled up. I stuck my thumb out and my eyes met Rod's, the EMT in Leather Pants, who was driving with the Latin cigar-smoking woman. He stopped, made some room and let me in. All the while he was filming me with a portable camera. He drove cautiously to the Convention Center, with the camera rolling, meandering through the streets with downed lines, trees, and scattered debris. He wanted to capture it all.

At the Convention Center there was a short line, requiring only an hour wait in the sun. An EMT asked about medical problems, and then the young men of the 82nd Airborne searched our bags. I mean really, *really* searched them. After another wait, this time under a canvas canopy, with free drinking water and cookies, we boarded a bus. Ahhhh. It was the first feeling of cool air in a week and a half. What a beautiful, cooling feeling. The war-torn, weary locals filed onto the bus, pets and all. Once filled, including five smelly dogs and a cockatiel on the shoulder of the woman in front of me, we pulled out of the lot and drove up the ramp over the Crescent City Connection (Greater New Orleans Bridge). It was disorienting, since I never would have taken this route to the airport.

I gave a longing look over the Mississippi River, flowing wide and easy and shimmering in the sun, then toward the French Quarter. I drank it in, since I knew it would have to last for a while.

"They're taking us to Belle Chase Naval Air Station," one evacuee reported confidently. "They must be." I hoped not.

But the driver continued on and then down Highway 90 on the Westbank. Although subdued, everyone on the bus eagerly surveyed the damage, which didn't seem to be as bad as we collectively had expected. But it was like dreaming just before you wake.

We soon pulled into the airport and to a surreal scene that I could never have visualized even after hundreds of trips to Louis Armstrong Airport: armed 82nd Airborne soldiers, empty cots and makeshift IVs, TSA and medical volunteers, most of them wearing surgical masks and gloves. Things moved in slow motion. My legs kept walking forward as I tried to unstick my mind.

After we went through a normal TSA airport screening, we were directed down the tarmac and I asked a soldier, "Where are we going? Where are we flying to?"

"I don't know sir. They don't tell us."

"OK, thanks."

"Sorry, sir."

I asked several more, and none of them could tell me. So finally, as they filed us into seats near a gate, I asked another, and he replied, "Wherever the pilot feels like going, sir. Honestly, they don't even tell us until we get on the plane."

"Where have they been going today?"

"Nashville, Charlotte, Salt Lake – all over."

"You're kidding. They don't tell us where we're going until we're on the plane?"

"No, sir. They really don't."

"Why?"

"I don't know, sir."

When a plane pulled in I was sure to get to the front of the line. I was going to get a first class seat. Nice and comfy. Problem was, they filled the plane from back to front, so I ended up in the back, next to the reeking restroom.

The planeload of passengers looked like none I'd ever seen, since, of course, these were mostly poor, mostly African-American folks – and probably three-quarters of them had never flown before.

Two armed guards, including one federal marshal in a bulletproof vest, stood with their hands on their weapons at the front of the plane. Two more were in the back near me. The man next to me, who was from Chalmette and had lost everything joked, "Welcome to Con Air." We had a little chuckle. Even the sickly African-American man next to him laughed. When we landed, he was carted off to the hospital.

The pilot came on the loudspeaker, "Welcome, folks. We'll be your crew today and it is our pleasure to serve you. We're going to the Greenville-Spartanburg, South Carolina Airport." My first thought was, "Where the hell's that?"

"Our flying time will be one hour and twenty minutes. Sit back, fasten your seatbelts and enjoy the ride."

I had just enough of a charge left on my cell phone to call my sister, Karen, and tell her. I didn't want to take the chance of getting stuck in Bumfuck Egypt. But apparently, the airport was only about two hours from their home in the north Atlanta suburbs, so my sister began to drive shortly after the plane took off.

We landed to a small contingent of reporters, politicians, and well-wishers. It was a welcome sight. As I passed them, a man smiled and drawled pleasantly, "Welcome to South Carolina, folks!" A woman offered a teddy bear to everyone, but I declined, since I thought the children on board would need them. Save them for the kids. But some of the adults took them too, and clutched them tightly.

We went through another TSA search inside and were shuffled off into buses. That was three searches so far and we'd been in the complete custody of military and Homeland Security officials the entire time. They weren't taking any chances after what had happened in the Superdome and at the Convention Center in New Orleans.

We walked out of the terminal toward a waiting bus. I could smell the perfume of a female volunteer as she pushed someone in a wheelchair ahead of me. "Darlin', you don't know how good it is to smell perfume."

"Oh, thank you, sir." Then she playfully offered her neck to me so I could fully inhale her scent. The back of my head tingled and we both giggled as we walked stride for stride.

We arrived at the Greenville Expo Center after a short ride with comments and jokes from the passengers like, "Gee, look at the hills here. It's like California," "I know we ain't in New Orleans, since there ain't no litter on the highway," and, "Can we stop for a Budweiser?"

Showers were set up in tents outside the Expo Center but I explained that I'd had one that morning. Others were coming out of the tents in scrubs, after cleaning up. Inside, clean air mattresses and a bevy of Red Cross workers greeted us. A beautiful young Latino woman in a Red Cross smock locked eyes with me and smiled broadly. I smiled back. I'd almost forgotten what it was like to exchange that look.

They had cold soft drinks, hot food and warm smiles. It wouldn't be so bad there – just no privacy. Those who were staying, which was everyone but me, didn't know how long they'd be there, but they seemed very happy to have a clean, cool, comfortable place - at last.

My sister arrived a half hour or so later as I finished a hot plate of food. I was leaving. The people of South Carolina were gracious, accepting and sympathetic and they were doing their level best to help. It was touching, to say the least. I felt immensely proud. We were all Americans, and they were really, really concerned for us. I felt humbled, since I hadn't felt I'd been through much, compared to most. Not like most of the people on the plane, and especially those in the 9th Ward and Chalmette who had lost their homes and everything in them. But it made me proud. Proud of how these people were helping, and proud of how these New Orleanians had held up.

We'd survived.

Chapter 11

After the Aftermath

The next day I slept in and then started watching CNN nonstop. It was much more frightening to watch on TV than to be there dealing with it. The dramatic music, the worst of the worst, over and over and over. And it was weird to see friends and locals being interviewed on national TV.

So I napped, ate, and stayed glued to the television the rest of the day. That night, I got my pictures developed. Even though I was still exhausted, I put up a blog with them and emailed as many friends and business associates as I could think of to let them know I was all right.

The following morning I went to my son's new school and gave them some legal papers and a copy of his birth certificate. Then it was back to the television, napping and eating to gain my strength back.

"You've got big bruises on your arms," my sister said, as I relaxed and extended them over my head, lying back on the sofa.

"Yeah, I think I fell on my bike. Could've been anything." I drifted back off to sleep.

The following Monday night was my son's open house at his new school. My sister and I went and met his teachers. Some of them had taught her three kids, who were now all enrolled at University of Georgia.

The next weekend, I flew to Chicago and Greg picked me up to drive to Iowa. We started on a cold 12-pack and talked nonstop all the way home. After dropping my things off at my mother's house, we went to meet a friend from high school, Dan Brown (our, "Brownie") and had a few at Governor's, a restaurant in our hometown, Bettendorf. Bettendorf is an unassuming bedroom community which sits on the Mississippi, across from Moline, 800 miles north of New Orleans.

The next day Greg and I drove to Iowa City to see the Hawkeyes play my alma mater, Northern Iowa. A scalper sold us some great seats, in the eighth row, on the 45 yard-line. It was a good game. For me, it was surreal to be there. Everyone's lives were perking along so... *normally.*

Then, on Sunday, it was my mother's 78th birthday, so I brought some flowers home for her. She'd probably prefer to say she's 39 for the second time.

On Sunday at church, I couldn't help but notice the faces from my past were a little more gray and drawn, but shining nevertheless. I hadn't been there in probably more than a decade. And although every face was Caucasian, an elder made it a point to mention that, "... although most of the people affected by the storm are not of the race we consider ourselves, as Christians, we seek to help them all, with grace and purity of heart."

Again, I was proud.

My mother and I went to a nice brunch at the Outing Club in Davenport. I ate an entire breakfast, then lunch. When we got home, I had to go to a trade association meeting in Chicago the next day, so I made the arrangements and left.

Things there were just fine in Chicago. It was a beautiful late summer day. People were happy. I had lunch out by the Navy Pier, which was calming. The water was a beautiful blue-green. I was OK.

Then a helicopter fluttered low and loud overhead, and my neck stiffened. In the distance, someone dropped something with a "CRACK" at the loading dock.

My first thought was, "Gunfire." I was still under a martial law mindset from New Orleans.

I shrugged off the neck pain and instant fever, then went back inside to the business conference. Maybe I wasn't completely over the aftermath. I needed something cool to drink. I got a Coke, and struggled through some more conference educational sessions.

That night, I went out with Bob Williams (the *fun* Bob Williams) and a few women; we got tanked after going to several parties. At the Houston ARMA chapter party, they were holding a raffle for Katrina victims. That was nice. Bob and I even won at pool at the Iron Mountain one. And we all danced at the wild Canadian party.

The next day, back at the hotel, I packed up and hailed a cab. I was leaving a little early. I was tired, and couldn't concentrate. The hangover from the night before would not quit.

As the taxi passed Madison Street, and then Orleans Street in downtown Chicago, I winced. Now I truly know what it means to miss New Orleans.

Epilogue

I was ready to get back to New Orleans after seven weeks in exile. Since one-way plane tickets from Atlanta were $500-$600, and Greyhound was only going as far as Hammond, I took an Amtrak train with a sleeping berth that left at 8:48 AM and was supposed to arrive at 7:20 PM. Three hot meals were included for under $100 total. Perfect. It was comfortable, and I was able to watch the countryside turn from Georgia clay to Cypress swamps while napping on and off and reading the New York Times.

The first thing I noticed when I got to the French Quarter were the refrigerators that lined the streets. People had left them with food that spoiled and smelled so bad they had to be thrown out. I really thought the place would be cleaned up by then, so it was distressing. The next thing I noticed were the abundance of New York State police. People say New Yorkers are so cold, but they are a generous and caring lot. They could really relate after what they went through with 9-11.

My apartment was pretty much in order. I'd left the light in the kitchen on, and after I'd cleaned my refrigerator out, I had plugged it back in, so there was cool water to drink. Still, no gas to cook with or take hot showers, though. I needed to get the line inspected and get the proper approvals.

I didn't even unpack. The first thing I did was to go check on Mr. Larry. He wasn't feeling well, so he was lying down in bed the whole time. He said that Michael had been shipped off to Colorado, but that he was back, and around somewhere. Chad, who had his Uptown apartment flooded, was there waiting on a hot date. He's a thirtyish party boy who had stayed with Mr. Larry through much of the aftermath once I'd left. He wanted to borrow a rubber so I gave him one of my Magnums. But the date stood him up so Chad and I went out to hit the Quarter bars, of which maybe 1/3 were open. We had a few beers at Razoo, the club where three white bouncers had strangled an African-American college kid earlier in the year. Now they hire scrawny bouncers. But it's usually hopping, and it was. I love going there to see sexy Ketris with the gravity-defying ass lead the crowd in singing and dancing. She's hot.

Then we went to Frenchmen Street to listen to some live music. The city still had 2 AM curfew, so we couldn't stay out too late. On the way home, we stopped at the "R Bar." A young bleach-blonde woman at the bar started talking with me. She wanted to know my name, but I wouldn't tell her (I don't know why), so she head-butted me a couple of times (not too hard). Well, that was an ice breaker. A half-hour later the three of us walked up Decatur and she stopped at Molly's on the Market to hug and kiss this real sexy brunette bartender. The bartender chick has sort of this Betty Boop thing going on, and she's covered with tattoos. After that, we walked a little further and the blonde girl turned around and lifted up her skirt, showing us that she had no panties on. I lightly stuck my finger in her pussy and brought it to my nose to smell it, and it was pretty sweet. Then she grabbed my finger and shoved it into her mouth, "I want to taste it!"

Back at my place, Chad ate her pussy and I played with her tits, and then they went to the back bedroom and I passed out. The next morning she was gone, but Chad said she could suck a mean dick.

So we headed over to Mr. Larry's in the morning, and I stopped in to see Armando and he gave me a free cigar. Mr. Larry still wasn't feeling well.

Chad wanted to go to the Voodoo Music Experience concert up at, "The Fly," which is on the river behind Audubon Park, Uptown. I talked a FEMA guy out of a ticket, and then grabbed a hot roast beef po-boy and we took a (free) bus ride up there.

It was great.

There were a lot of creative T-shirts, like "Got Mold?" "Screw Falujah, Rebuild New Orleans!" and "ReNEW ORLEANS." It was great to see so many people celebrating New Orleans. It was great to see all those beautiful young women, and it was a great day without a cloud in the sky. Fred, the drummer for Cowboy Mouth led what was like sort of a massive group therapy session – for 20,000 people. We were all screaming and singing along with him, "Let it go, let it go, let it go… let it go, let it go, let it GO!" And they debuted a song that waxed poetic about New Orleans, "…and the bands will play, and the parades will roll again… on the Avenue…" Tears streamed down my face.

Queens of the Stone Age played next, and they were pretty good. Then we ran into Mad Mike. He'd been in Houston and had just gotten back, so he fired up a joint of Houston pot. We drank some beers and shot the breeze, just catching up. After Nine Inch Nails started, I ended up going to Cooter Brown's for a few more and I'd lost Chad somewhere in the shuffle. Oh yeah, I remember now: this woman came and grabbed my hand and pulled me toward the stage. When she sat down I saw she didn't have any panties on, and she had a neatly trimmed patch. I'm pretty sure she showed me on purpose.

Yes, I was back in New Orleans!

The following afternoon, I ran into Harry Anderson at the A&P. That was unusual, since he's more of a Matassa's kind of guy. He said he didn't really have a rally, just a town hall meeting at his club. I told him he was in the book, and he said, "Good! I'm glad I made the cut!"

I noticed a crowd forming in the street when I walked home. Louis Sahuc, the photographer, had a book signing for a Galatoire's cookbook outside his studio and they blocked off the street on Chartres and served free wine and shrimp remoulade. I was wondering where the shrimp came from, but it sure was good. Then, at around three o'clock or so, I went over to a party that socialite Margarita Bergen was having in the Marigny. She's known for her fancy hats. She had food (even gumbo!), drinks, a bartender, and a band playing New Orleans classics. There was an odd mix of old money, transvestites and Saints fans (they lost – again).

And we were all back. Just in time for Halloween!

Part II

Pre-K.

(Pre-Katrina)

Life in the French Quarter before Hurricane Katrina hit on August 29, 2005, from a blog I had started in the spring of 2005.

Tuesday, April 12, 2005

Mad Mike, Bell & French Quarter Fest

Two nights ago I treated myself to wet Absolut martinis and a thick filet (medium, with bourbon sauce) at Dickie Brennan's Steakhouse.

Sure, put it on the account.

Things are good.

I figured this is big. Or at least it will be, when I figure out what it is.

The steak melted in my mouth like butter that had been out on the kitchen table on a hazy August afternoon – with the air conditioning off.

I had never done it, it was totally out of my realm, but I the staged reading of my first play – ever– the first weekend in April. Yeah, I wrote a play! It was sort of divine intervention - I'll tell you about Henry H. later. It was a surreal experience, to hear my words come to life. Some of the actors were so good they made the words better. People who came... uh... the few, seemed to genuinely enjoy the three performances, which began April 1. Hmmmm.

Well, anyway, a clownish but very intelligent friend of mine would've had his 47th birthday on April Fool's, except that he died in his sleep in December. So long, Greg Bell. You were a good buddy. Peace.

OK, that was uplifting! But, hey, Bell is probably laughing from above. He used to joke so much he used to say he wanted a clown nose on him at his funeral, so that people could pass by the casket and honk it! So Greg wouldn't want anyone to mourn too long, or especially to lose their sense of humor. And on his trips to the oilfields of Nigeria, he would pack his bags with clothes for the orphans, and sometimes he read to them. It helped him out of a scrape when some insurgents held Greg and his men hostage, "You are the American that reads to the children?"

"Yes."

"You can wait inside in the air-condition."

But Greg Bell refused and stayed with his men.

The guy evolved, I mean *really* evolved.

Let's go on to lighter subjects, like Hunter Thompson blowing his brains out, Dostoyevsky's prescription for happiness, or Dukowski's ball-eating, or what? So if you get those references - or at least one - then you're in the right place.

Or if you like to have a good time listening to live music, socializing, laughing, drinking, and enjoying your life – like we do here in New Orleans.

"No man is a failure, who is enjoying life." - *William Faulkner*

Or, if you just want the truth. Read on.

My play: I've been rewriting the thing hard for the last three days. I think I cut about 10 pages and added about 14. So it's getting better. I thought it was perfect, until I saw it done at the live reading, and I still thought it was pretty good, but then we did this script review meeting with a couple of actor/directors (Dane Rhodes and Liz) and I took lots of notes and listened a lot. Now I'm cranking - with new things to consider. It's a lot of fun. The best.

This is my right brain stuff, my interest in literature, theatre and the arts. I remember in high school we learned this basic sentence in Latin class (thank you, Magister Buhr) that translated into this: *Life is short, art is long.* So it finally hit me – in my forties - that I'd better learn about and pursue the arts, and maybe contribute to them, if I was going to get into something that, "mattered." So I wrote my novel, *Jackson Squared*, wrote my play, *Brando, Tennessee & Me*, and came up with a Mafia screenplay idea that I have some interested parties looking at. In fact, I received a Letter of Intent for it from a Wall Strret film capital fund, which said they'd put $3-5M into it! So maybe I can do this writing thing.

Oh, and also I cranked up my writing for computer magazines which I do as an extension of consulting and speaking on content, document and knowledge management technologies and methods. So the day after my last play production, which was during the Tennessee Williams Festival here (that I pitched in and volunteered for, third year, I love it), yes, the day after I had two articles due on collaborative software. I blasted them out but didn't quite get the second one done - but they gave me some extra time.

And then last weekend was French Quarter Fest here in the Quarter! My FAVORITE fest! It's great. Better than Jazz Fest, but don't tell anyone. Local music, great food, a little shade, a view of the river, and cold beer. Oh, and port-o-lets, when I didn't want to go back a block away to my place in the heart of the Quarter.

Bluesman Coco Robichaux, part Cajun, part Native American, all heart and one of my favorite local singer/musicians, was great. The crowd gave him a lot of love, and he said, "I'm still reelin' from it," when he came down from the stage, staggering from the appreciation he'd received. Sexy singer Irene Sage, who I had a big crush on years ago, sang backup.

The Five People You Meet in Hell: Surviving Katrina

Henry Butler was great too. Now there's a guy - he's an outstanding photographer (and great singer/musician) and he's been blind since birth! Yep! Look into it.

Now to words. Tonight continues the semi-annual, "Festival of the Imagination," at the Goldmine Saloon. It's a great collection of poetry, spoken word, and some music and art. It's a cool thing that Dave Brinks is doing. But I'm beat: been laying around since I double-dosed on pilates and yoga today, and also did a morning walk. I'll go tomorrow night. Hmmm… maybe it was going out last night and seeing Mad Mike at Checkpoint Charlie's. It was open mike night, & Mad Mike was wide open.

He's a very subversive-folk-comic-singer-banjo/guitar player - a little over the top but funny as hell. Last night, he sang some of his original songs, "Let's Get the Baby High," and, "I Love the Devil," but the one that I think drove away the hot fetish model chick, (Claire, with pink fishnets on!) was the one about all the STDs he'd gotten from a girl, and how he still loved her. (Boy, that Claire was squirmin'!)

Mad Mike (he calls himself "the hippie bum") was stumbling pretty bad once his pills kicked in. He was celebrating an inheritance of some sort.

And sexy cute April at CC's coffeehouse, don't think I haven't noticed that tongue ring! I know it was your birthday, and baby, you were beaming!

Thursday, April 14, 2005

Tuba Fats, Down by the River & More

Tuba Fats was this great guy - a tuba player, obviously - who kept the live traditional jazz scene in Jackson Square going for years. He died a year ago January. He was a gentle soul who lived a block away from me in the Quarter, and he always had time to say, "hi" and chat a bit. He did that with almost everyone.

He walked tall - he was a good 400 pounds with plump catcher's mitt hands, and if things got a little out of hand with the street musicians, or the other local urchins and homeless folks, he knew when to step in. Once I heard him say to a guy, "Now, you wouldn't want to get an ass-whuppin' over that, would you?", 'nuff said.

Anyway, the guy had the greatest jazz funeral ever, with the crowds swelling more and more as the Second Line (a New Orleans dance, sort of like the hokey-pokey and bunny hop with waiving white handkerchiefs and twirling parasols) filled the streets of the French Quarter after leaving Gallier Hall (that's also where Harry Connick, Jr. was married) on St. Charles Avenue. I saw my good friend and writer Barber, an English professor from Auburn who comes down to drink and write. I waved as I second-lined on down the street. Barber was dead by the end of the year. Tragic. But his fatal heart attack came while while doing what he loved – teaching a class. That's probably the way he would've wanted it.

This morning I wasn't in much of a good mood, but they played a Tuba Fats song on WWOZ, the greatest radio station on the planet (and you can listen from anywhere at wwoz.org) and it lightened my mood. I loved Tuba.

After his funeral, I helped hoist his casket from the horse-drawn carriage into the hearse - an honor - and the entire crowd - black, white, European, Asian, whatever, continued into the Tremé (Trem-may) area where he grew up, to have a party. People were drinking, smoking, singing, shouting and dancing in the streets. I left just before dark: just before some guy with leg braces got shot and killed by a bar owner for selling beer outside his bar. The bar owner later died in jail.

Here's a poem I wrote for Tuba, which I left at the makeshift altar in the seat of the bench in where he used to sit and play:

<u>SWEET TUBA FATS</u>

Tuba, Tuba

You dear sweet man!

Bouncing a toddler, gently

on your

big knee,

and smiling -

then om-pah bass notes

for the crowd

gathering

Making their day

And their stay

And the world

Happier

Softer

Brighter

The Five People You Meet in Hell: Surviving Katrina

Grander

And today I heard

you passed on,

a kinder man

won't come along

Jackson Square

the Quarter

the music

the world

Will never be

What it was

without you

playing

singing

saying…

Your bigness

Your love

Your generosity

Made New Orleans

A better city

God knows

You did

your part -

There never was

A bigger heart.

Thanks for the love and memories Tuba, we miss you!

So anyway - yesterday's steak has turned into peanut butter, and the bill for last month's steak arrived in the mail. Am I an optimist or an idiot?

I'm waiting to get paid for a computer article I wrote 6 months ago and it was finally published the first of April. Half the money's gone, OK - ALL of it, but half of it's gone to pay the actors for my play-reading. I kind of got stuck unexpectedly with that by the producer. Yeah, that's the price of progress, if you want it that bad. I still owe a couple of guys.

How about some divine intervention? Hey, I'm working hard here!

To lift my spirits I took a walk along the Mississippi River - it's only a block away, and the fog horns at night put me to sleep, just like they did when I was a kid living 800 miles upriver, less than a mile from the river in my little Iowa hamlet. ZZZZzzzzzzzzzzz.

When you walk along and see the happy tourists devouring beignets or strolling with their kids, you see smiles and you hear laughter. Then the toot-tooting of the calliope (sort of steam-powered organ) starts at exactly 10:45 every morning from the Steamboat *Natchez*, and there are more happy tourists.

I passed by the guy who was giving Mad Mike the pills the other night, but he didn't recognize me. He was wearing this funny Mexican blanket as a skirt, the kind that you'd see draped over the back of a burro. He was unshaven and dazed, looking like he'd been on a 5-day binge. Oh yeah, he's a writer too!

Then through Jackson Square, and children gleefully chasing pigeons. I had the real urge to join the guy on the park bench with a quart of beer, but thought I'd never make it to the Festival of the Imagination tonight if I did. Besides, I've got stuff to do.

Friday, April 15, 2005 **Festival of the Imagination, 'No Legs' James & Rosecart Bobby; Gutter Punk Gets His Ass Kicked**

So after I was spent, braindead, I made the genius decision to have a 24-oz. Miller High Life and listen to the music in Jackson Square anyway. That started it. Call me Einstein.

Mark, who has replaced Tuba Fats on the tuba (actually he plays a dented, duct-taped sousaphone), Andy, the string bass player with a rag on his head to block the sun, and the rest of the brass and drums ensemble started out a little after 2 PM with a rousing rendition of, "We Danced All Night." And literally, within five minutes, there were 100 people gathered around, tapping their toes, smiling, and dancing. These guys have redefined the word, "ragtag." But they have heart.

"This is good. This is a good day, right here in Jackson Square," I thought.

My worries were gone - temporarily.

So after an afternoon of beer, smiles, and pee, I headed down Royal St. and saw "No Legs" James and "Rosecart" Bobby on the corner.

Bobby runs the business that sells roses on Bourbon Street, and James, who had his legs amputated after years of being a long-haul trucker, sells roses for Bobby quite successfully from his wheelchair on Bourbon at Orleans.

Late one afternoon I drank a bottle of cheap vodka with James and Lisa, the "Crazy Contentious Pollack" (but educated – she's finishing her PhD), along the river as the sun set slowly behind the GNO bridge. We ended up a little rowdy and drinking beer at Harry's Bar on Chartres after dark. James likes to gamble, so he would periodically wheel over to the video poker machine, between arguments. The guy may have no legs, but he's still full of fire. He said he knows why God put him on this earth - to show people you can still work even if you don't have any legs. We've gotten along pretty well (after that); poor James, now they're starting to cut off his fingers because of the diabetes. James lives at the same old folks home that Henry H., did, only James was always more self-sufficient. Oh yeah, James is black.

I always had to take care of Henry, until he died in December, the day after Greg Bell did. I found out after I'd gone to the Abbey Bar to celebrate Greg's life with a cold beer. Then Gracie told me Henry died. Damn! Two friends gone in two days! And my friend Barber had dropped dead in front of his English class at Auburn the month before. Damn it.

Back to James… he not only gambles, but he likes the ladies too. My favorite line was when he said, "Hell, I still got one leg!"

That's a little freaky, I hate that picture. Poor guy, he used to be a mountain of a man, six-two or six-three, and now he's dick-high to everyone. But he still has pride, so we should all think about that.

So Bobby and No Legs James and I sat on the corner and mostly gawked and commented on the women. Bobby wants to bang this nutty art woman who's an art gallery owner. She's so flighty - and she's married - that it never crossed my mind before.

So here's Bobby - bird-dogging women, while he's showing me the wound where a hunk of flesh was taken from the inside of his cheek that afternoon for a biopsy. He was hurting, so James gave him a Tylenol #3. Bobby's already beaten throat cancer, so I hope he's alright. Nice guy, interesting and funny guy, and he employs the unemployable. The first time I met him was at Mardi Gras, and he was completely done-up in theatrical make-up as a monkey-man. Funny as all get out. He said all the gay guys kept asking to see his gorilla cock.

And while we were kidding around, I noticed the gutter punk that I kicked the shit out of a few months ago, sitting on a garbage can catty-corner from us, just eyeing us, in between reading a book. I thought, "You can't read, gutter punk-boy. Who are you kidding?!"

Usually now when I see him he just looks away or looks down, and goes the other way.

Yeah, a few months ago, this smelly fucker sits down next to me at my usual spot at Flanagan's. I go there because the beer's cheap. But also, I've seen Nicolas Cage, Lisa Marie Presley and Billy from ZZ Top there. Even talked with Billy. He said, "Hmm. Funny. Same three chords for twenty-five years. I can't explain it." I had to laugh. I mean, I always liked their music, especially, "Pearl Necklace." (Ha haa). I didn't want to bug Nick Cage, I like his acting but I'm sure people like that just want a little space sometimes, just to hang out. I don't have that problem: all I do is hang out.

So gutter punk is killing my buzz with his noxious fumes, and I politely ask him to move to the other side of the bar. He replies with a, "Fuck you." So I asked him again and got the same response. Then I told him I was going to the bathroom and he'd better be on the other side of the bar when I get back. He says another "Fuck You!" and then, this dumbass says to me, "Take your best shot." Well, the split second he says, "shot," I leaped out of my chair and hit him with a left cross, followed by a sharp right (just like Pop taught me) and then left-right-left-right-left-right – a flurry of maybe 30 punches to the head, as he tried to duck for cover. I had to resort to uppercuts to keep pummeling his face. His ugly-ass girlfriend was there, with her tattooed face, and I look down and she's squeezing my balls from under the bar and looking up at me fiendishly, while I'm pounding the shit out of him. It didn't really hurt. I like my fat balls squeezed. Thanks, you dirty stinking whore.

It was like an Irish three-way!

Then she bites me in my left leg – hard. I had shorts on, so she got a big chunk - and then somebody grabs me from behind and pulls me backwards, and the kid gets up and takes one cheap shot to my right eye. Then, a kick to my ribs. I shook it off, got up, REALLY pissed off, and he ran around to the back of the bar. Tattoo Andy, the bar manager, came up and gently escorted me out. I found out later that Andy's boyfriend (a tough fruit?) had grabbed me, which I don't begrudge, because when you run a bar you have to keep order. Funny thing was, the bar was full of tourists waiting to go on a ghost tour. Extra show for them, no charge. I found out the next day that stinky gutter-punk boy works for Andy at the bar. Oh, and I didn't have to pay my tab. Nice.

I've thought about retaliating for that cheap shop, but after I heard about his black eyes and all, I figured he'd had enough. Besides, he knows, since now he won't even look me in the eye. The next day I had a strained bicep from the extreme uppercuts, and jammed knuckles, and a sore left side. No big deal. I won. I've still got it. Punk-ass bitch.

Yesterday, then, after hanging out I headed over to the Goldmine, good and drunk, to listen to the poetry and spoken word. Dave Brinks was very gracious in welcoming me. It's cool what he's doing, since he records everything on video tape and in 50 or 100 years, poets and the public will be able to see this scene, and the evolution of the words. I honestly like Dave's poetry. It's the poetry of a man who had a happy and secure childhood (what's THAT like?), and it's just peaceful and light. And very good, very lyrical and innovative.

The walls of the dank saloon (former horse stable) were covered with the art exhibit from Tuesday. It wasn't quite as crowded as last year, maybe since Andrei Codrescu wasn't reading. He's in New York, on his way to the Middle East to do research for a book he's doing. Codrescu is pretty cool. He's funny as hell in person, he likes to drink and shoot the shit, and I think he challenges his students to reach much higher than they thought they could go. Codrescu's sort of a mentor, and good friend, to Brinks. But to be Codrescu's friend, you have to be able to withstand his constant Eastern European barbs and harsh humor. He does it all in a funny way, though.

The performance opened with an Asian woman singing beautifully, followed by a black man reading angry, meaningful poetry. Later, Dave's wife read something sort of sexual or gross about menses and a dog licking the blood or something. I finished my second beer, which I was short 15 cents on, but Bill Myers let me slide. Then he served up a couple of waters to keep me occupied (and hydrated?).

The best thing about it, though, was that I stayed and watched a younger kid do his reading. He was pretty good. He's probably 19 or so, and goes by "Nero." He was one of those few who went to see my play the week before. Michael the Artist, who hangs out at Royal and Orleans sketching images of the St. Louis Cathedral and drinking oil cans of Foster's, brought Nero to the play reading. Apparently, Nero had been going through one of those suicidal-writer sort of phases, and he coughed throughout my play like he had a new case of TB. And now, because he saw my play, he's writing one. He's writing again! Ain't that cool? Outside, when I congratulated him, he was on a cell phone, and he told the caller, "I'm shaking hands right now - with a playwright!" Maybe I *am* a playwright now?

I wrote a few poems when I got home, then fell asleep with my legs hanging over the loveseat, only to be awakened by my boisterous teenager, (my pride and joy, really) barging through the balcony doors at 1 AM. He does that when the door is locked, since he always loses his keys. I guess he was working late at McDonald's and he had a school project due so came over to use up all the colored ink in my printer.

<u>Sunday, April 17, 2005</u> Bruce Almighty, Dioxin-face & Friendly Bar

Well, well, well. I'm sitting here hung over after the weekend, and let's see what comes out. I'm sipping my Cool Brew ice coffee and trying to recollect. I took my morning walk both days on the weekend along the Mississippi. One day, some guy was actually fishing down by the

Governor Nicholls Street Wharf which is akin to Homer Simpson fishing in the haz mat runoff outside the nuclear power plant.

Further down toward the Aquarium Saturday, a gaggle of high school cheerleaders practiced in Woldenberg Park. It reminded me of the time when I was in high school, maybe a freshman, and the cheerleaders were practicing at Diane Drexler's house, which was one off from being catty-corner from my backyard in Iowa. They actually wanted me to watch them to see how they were doing. It was Dawn Rutherford, Diana Freeman, Laura Esping, Drexler, and a few others. Boy, what I would've given to get into their limber, sweaty pussies! About 20 years later I did bang one of them a couple of times. She was house-sitting and we hit the liquor cabinet pretty hard and had two nights of blurred ecstasy.

Another subject: yesterday I got a glimmer of good news. Finally R.E. returned an email about negotiations on my screenplay. I went to the Writer's Guild (WGA) site and found out that the standard rate is somewhere between $50K-$100K, and that progress payments are made as you turn in the treatment, the first draft etc. So I've been working on this for four months - much longer than I thought it'd take, and I need some damn money for it.

Interesting how A.E. likes my Cajun Mafia vs. Italian Mafia movie idea. He's half Cajun, and half Italian, and his uncle was the most notorious mob boss in New Orleans – Carlos Marcello. In fact, the Mafia began in

New Orleans, since a lot of Sicilians landed here. Also, another relative of his was a popular Cajun politician. But he's not where I originally got the idea - it was actually from R.M., the wild-ass Cajun lawyer from Lafayette who was the largest contributor to the crooked governor's campaign two times in a row (and oh, incidentally, won the largest two personal injury awards in Louisiana history. A connection?). I met R.M. in Schellas' barber shop in Bourbon Street. R.M.'s a writer now. He's very intense, and we ended up going next door and drinking super sweet pink lemonade (he's recovered) while he told me stories for hours. He's big with the Running of the Bulls in Pamplona and wrote a book on it. He has all sorts of stories about drug dealers, the Gagliano gang (the old men all went to prison, now the kids run Frank's Place that the Feds bugged and caught them plotting murders). Anyway, R.M. must be into something, since he moved permanently to the French countryside last year. He said something about Interpol harassing him when he travels overseas, since he's in the system as a suspected drug money courier. He spends winters in Mexico, and blows through town now and then. A little suspicious, eh?

With the good news that A.E. is coming into town Tuesday, I skipped into Jackson Square. Dealer Tommy and Patty were out there. Patty cleans my place when I have the money. I headed up to the corner of Royal and Toulouse (too-loose) outside the Supreme Court building where Bruce Almighty, or Bruce the Tarot Reader, was scamming tourists with phony palm readings and Tarot. It's funny to see him tell everyone the same thing! Bruce was packing up, and I played with Trinky, the wiener dog Bruce inherited from his skanky girlfriend's dead mother. We headed over to his place, which is a one-room apartment above Chris Owens' Club. The music thumps loud as hell through the floor, and it blares in the window from the Bourbon Street Blues Company across the street. Chris Owens has been an exotic dancer/entertainer for like 50 years. Although she's getting a little long in the tooth, she's still has nice legs! She's such an icon here that she has her own Easter parade, and sometimes she rides with the sheriff on a Mardi Gras float.

Bruce's alcoholic-scag girlfriend was just waking up. She bitched and moaned as she waddled to a chair, while I poured her a stiff rum and Coke. This woman is so ugly she looks like she o.d.'d on dioxin. One drunken night, Bruce, who's had prostate cancer, gets out his little peter and pumps it up (yes, literally, he has one of those penis pumps implanted) and starts sticking it into her mouth. And I had to watch. Yick!

What a skanky-ugly-bitch-slut.

Of course, Bruce Almighty and Dioxin-face commence to arguing, as usual, and she tells him to leave. They take turns hitting each other and calling the cops and sending the other to jail. It's ridiculous, and dangerous - I'm afraid one of them is going to kill the other in a drunken rage.

So Bruce locks the half-gallon of Bacardi in his safe and he and I head over to Fahey's to shoot some pool. Bruce steps in to the Corner Pocket by mistake, which is a gay bar a block away from Fahey's. I was laughing my ass off - kidding Bruce that people must've thought we were a couple! The only time I'd been in that bar was a few weeks ago when some couple found me on the Internet and wanted me to fuck the wife. The guy described her as 5'7" and 130, Italian. Sounds pretty good, huh? But man, was she UGLY! Hook-nose. And drunk as hell. She was grabbing the scrawny gay dancers' cocks and all. Creepy. We left and she was doing that 'stagger-fall-plop-sit down' stupid-ass routine, so nothing ever happened. I was curious, but it was just a waste of time and a pretty creepy.

Bruce and I found Fahey's and we had a good game of pool. He can actually play whereas I have to concentrate really hard to keep from getting bored. Then a couple of guys played us and they were whipping us until they scratched. I'm not sure what happened after that, except that I stopped in at Funky Pirate on Bourbon and saw Grace, a 70-something friend of mine who is a waitress there. She goes to church every day, but she works as a waitress to get extra money to put her granddaughter through law school. Oh, that reminds me - I saw Cokie Roberts' mom (Lindy Boggs) in the A&P today in her Sunday best. She's this tiny little lady. I met her last year, she's so lively and positive, encouraging and sweet! No wonder Cokie's so down-to-earth. I decided not to bother Miss Lindy, though.

And Grace is such a pleasant and genuinely sweet person - and she bought me a beer. So I sat and talked with her in-between her waiting on tables. Then I woke up at home.

Friday I went out with my lesbian friend, Henrietta. Sometimes we alternate going to gay and straight bars, sort of like I used to with my dearly-departed brother, Bill. We decided to go into The Friendly Bar in the Marigny. We were immediately accosted by a septuagenarian queen, who talked about how to pronounce "Marigny" (Mare-i-knee) for like ten fucking minutes. The average age in the place was probably 60 plus. Henrietta said it's the same people, only 25 years and 25 pounds later. Lots of high school gym teacher-looking old lesbians and slump-shouldered, testosterone-challenged queens. And lots of laughter actually. It *is* a Friendly Bar. So we had a few laughs and a few beers.

Then we went to the R Bar, over on Royal in the Marigny. Jonathan Ferrara, the art gallery owner, just bought it a few months ago. It's a pretty cool place - casual, with a nice vibe. Henrietta starts with this frat boy routine like, "Hey man, where's the fucking pussy?"

So we had a few more laughs.

Well, gotta get some real work done.

I should get a steady job and stop living life, eh? Naw. Time is everything.

Monday, April 18, 2005 **Wanna See My Movie?**

I switched one of the scenes around, and it works a little better. Since I had that script review meeting with the actor/directors for my play, and had a couple of conversations with Perry Martin about dialogue, I think it's actually helping me on the screenplay. I hadn't looked at it in a month, since I was waiting on feedback from Chris, the screenwriter in NYC who A.E. paired me up with to make the project "bankable," (since this is my first one).

The formatting is a little fucked up, since the text editor on this blog site sucks.

You want Sex & Violence? OK, first scene, right out of the box. Oh, and I'm open to someone else optioning this right now.

MOB VS. MOB

A screenplay by Robert F. Smallwood

April 2005

EXT. BARBADOS BEACH RESORT -- DAY

TITLE CARD: "BARBADOS, 1968"

The beach is an ideal scene filled with scantily-clad, beautiful women and men. Some of the women are topless. A small group plays volleyball and others enjoy a board game over drinks.

C.U. BARECHESTED MAN IN CHAISE LOUNGE CHAIR SIPPING
AN UMBRELLA DRINK IN THE BRIGHT SUN. HIS FACE IS
HIDDEN.

The man sips the drink, calmly setting it back in its holder and breathes a contented sigh. Suddenly bullets shatter the drink glass and tear open his torso as he is riddled with dozens of shots, jumping and jerking from the impact. Chaos erupts. A group of assassins run off the beach into a waiting speedboat that shoots rooster tails of water as it speeds away.

INT. NAPOLEON HOUSE, NEW ORLEANS — NIGHT

A group of Italian men meet in a darkened corner, dressed in 1960s-style gangster fashions. They talk quietly.

MOB BOSS DIBERNARDO

Yeah, like 'Silver Dollar' used to say, "Time to

put a Stoppagherra to this."

DIBERNARDO ASSOCIATE

Yeah, 'three can keep a secret if two's dead...'

The group snickers and laughs gutturally.

MOB BOSS DIBERNARDO

You got it. Now Giuseppe, you an' Dog Face take

care of it. All right?

DOG FACE

They done, boss. They done.

INT. MONTELEONE HOTEL BALLROOM, NEW ORLEANS --
NIGHT

GOVERNOR CHAMPAGNE is celebrating his election with campaigners
and friends. BOBBY CHAMPAGNE, JOCK SPARTACHINO, LAWYER
DUPRÉ, and TOMMY HEBERT are nearby. Armed guards stand behind
Governor Champagne.

GOVERNOR CHAMPAGNE

How y'all are?

The crowd responds with collective cheers and laughter.

GOVERNOR CHAMPAGNE (CONT'D)

It's so good to see you all here. We won! We

won! How's about that?

Governor Champagne pauses as the crowd cheers him. He gives a signal to the crowd with his forefinger and pinkie extended. He waves at BENNIE DOUVET, an older African-American man (Morgan Freeman-like), and winks. Bennie Douvet waves and raises his clapping hands in return as he nods approvingly.

GOVERNOR CHAMPAGNE (CONT'D)

Yes, yes, thank you. Thanks to everyone who

worked so hard on the campaign. From Shreveport

and Monroe, to Lake Charles, Baton Rouge, here

in New Orleans and even down in Grand Isle,

thanks to all the folks who supported us. And to

my good friends down in Acadiana, thank you.

Vous remercier encore pour tout votre soutien! Je

vraiment l'apprécie. And I won't forget you when

it comes time to put that highway all the way through

to Lafayette! And we'll sell some of that extra rice

you got overseas. We'll help out our sugar cane

farmers too! Like Huey Long said, "Every man a

king!" Ah – eee!

Cheers from the audience interrupt him.

GOVERNOR CHAMPAGNE (CONT'D)

...and thanks again to our good friends here in New

Orleans. We surely do appreciate your support and we

always, ALWAYS enjoy coming to New Orleans!

Mob Boss DiBernardo waves from among the supporters. He is smoking a cigar and surrounded by young women, with DiBernardo Associate and Dog Face keeping a watchful eye.

GOVERNOR CHAMPAGNE (CONT'D)

And of course I'd like to be the first to congratulate

Lieutenant Governor DeGrazio. Now let's just enjoy

this evening and our victory celebration! Le bon

ton roulé!

Governor Champagne leaves the podium and begins making his way through it shaking hands. Bodyguards press close to him, keeping an eye out. The crowd begins eating hors d'oeuvres and drinking champagne from trays that waiters circulate.

Wednesday, April 20, 2005

Harry Anderson, Pug Elvis & still...

I saw Harry Anderson going into his place on the way to my post office box this afternoon. He was the judge on "Night Court" and he's my neighbor. He's mainly a magician and claims not to be an actor, but he's funny as hell. Once we were talking in a store close to his house and he puts the owner's (more on Mick later) pug dog on his head and says, "Look! Pug Elvis!" The dog's tail curled down his forehead like Elvis' hair, and the little legs angled down the side of his face like Elvis' porkchop sideburns. It was fucking hilarious! Sometimes Harry comes in to Flanagan's Bar to buy cigarettes or drink (Mount Gay) rum and cokes. We talk about the Quarter, politics and also the TV/movie business a little. He's a cool guy and always entertaining. And his wife is very pretty. He's opening up a club on the corner of Esplanade and Decatur to do his magic and comedy act. I gave him the script for my play and he said it'd be perfect to do at his club, since he's built a stage and it holds about 100 in sort of a dinner theatre setting. So maybe that's a way to get my play out there sooner. Back to Mick, the store owner. He keeps hiring these strung out gutter punks. Word is that middle-aged Mick with the growing pot belly has a thing for these young, skinny, gutter punk guys. He even shot up heroin with one of them to try to get the guy to fall in love with him. That's a little extreme, eh?

Hey, in one week, I've written enough for about 1/10 of a book on here. Maybe this is my next book? Hmmm. No, gotta get the novel out first.

Thursday, April 21, 2005

Jazz Fest is Here

It's Jazz Fest weekend, or, "Invasion of the Middle-Aged Hippies." which is always a good time. It's more of a hassle than French Quarter Fest, it's packed and a drag to get up and trudge through the crowds to go to the bathroom, but there are big acts and it's a good time for locals and tourists alike. I'm sure Fat Bastard and Organic Annie will be there, as usual, with smuggled bottles of booze, joints, and a great appreciation for the tunes!

Saturday, April 23, 2005

Just Plodding Along

Well, yesterday was a tough day. Business and personal-wise.

Just tried to handle it with grace. I've been in pain since Sunday, since I did a big weight workout at the gym at the Sheraton and I've been sore. Actually Friday I did this 45-minute step/cardio/boot camp class with Wendell and I was hobbling all weekend. Getting trashed with Bruce

Almighty didn't help either. Just made it worse. And my neck is killing me from the stress and probably sitting at the computer.

Sometimes it seems like a beheading would be a relief.

My friend Larry's Dad died - his wife Belinda left a message.

Cremation, no service.

I woke up at 4 AM this morning, then at almost 6, so I decided to get up.

Yesterday, I had three interviews scheduled for my article on IT in the pharmaceutical industry, one of which would also cover digital rights management (DRM).

I shot a quick email to the PR firm and told them to call on the other line. The reply came back and things went swimmingly with the iLumin folks. Only they're a little short on installations, so I can't give them much ink.

I took my riverside walk. Nice day. I keep seeing this guy who looks like Brad Pitt on a 14-day meth binge. Saturday he asked me what day it was. Friday? Saturday? When you're homeless, it doesn't much matter. Oh, I also saw the writer/nutcase who has been giving Mad Mike the pills. He's now completely shaved his head, and he looks like a new Hare Krishna recruit. Complete with the glazed look.

As I readied for the noontime interview, I discovered - to my horror - that my Internet connection was down.

Now what? I've got Voice over IP! I need the Internet!

This one was a call-in conference call anyway, so I hustled over to Armando's cigar shop and the wooden Indian wasn't outside, meaning he was closed. I went anyway, and he was just leaving to park his car, so he ran in a grabbed his phone. Good guy. He's in recovery. (Not for me).

Whew, made it through that. Now what for the 1 o'clock interview with Liquid Machines?

Oddly, I flipped the TV on, and it was back - so the cable and Internet was on! So they called and everything was cool.

I decided to treat myself, so I charged some escargot and a salad, and a few beers and martinis at Palace Cafe and Dickie Brennan's. When things are the worst, it's the Brennan's to the rescue! I've had accounts with them for 15 years. I just want to get through the day is all. With some enjoyment.

Can't stand the stress. I need some money for that screenplay! I should crank up the consulting too. That's good money. I was pulling down $200K+ each year (that's like a million, in New Orleans). Before I started this writing thing. And I only worked 25-30 hours a week, but traveled a lot.

Yippee there's a new Pope. He looks just like the other guy. He was in the Hitler Youth and manned a gun in an airplane for Nazi Germany (but he did desert: give him a little credit). And he's an arch-conservative. Great. Makes sense. Don't get me wrong, I'm not Catholic, but I do think John Paul II was a genuinely good person. Just inflexible, and really, he presided over all the cover-up and moving child-molesting priests around. The new one is 78 so he'll croak soon. It's funny to see those guys and their smoke signals and cute-sy red, gold, and white costumes. It seems like they're just an elaborate bunch of Webelos or real dyke-y Campfire Girls or something with their ridiculous get-ups. That ritualistic stuff is freaky. And then there's the pedophilia, and pedophilia cover-up. And all that money, hierarchical power and, well, it just seems so, so **man-made**, *so full of motives.*

Monday, May 9, 2005

Mother's Day at Johnny White's

So I was out in Jax Square again Sunday, and I ran in to Christine and her mom - they were at the benefit at Antoine's Friday, where I performed two scenes from my play - invited me to go for a beer. So with one on each arm, we went to Johnny Whites and had a few beers. Christine's mom was talking about her as a little girl, and teenager, and how much trouble she got in. I guess she used to scare her (gay) brother when she'd knock on his window to try to sneak back in at night.

Christine and her mom are almost like sisters. They have about the same build and both smoke like chimneys, but I think Christine likes to gossip even more.

It was fun, but Christine sort of was chiding me about the business of my writing - like I don't know what I'm fucking doing. I explained it to her somewhat, but she doesn't really know the whole picture. It was flattering that she thinks I've really got something. But I don't really like all that nosiness. It was hard for me to defend since I've invested everything in the writing, to the expense of practicality, which was why they were buying the beers that afternoon. It was sort of like my kid saying, "If you're so smart, how come you're not rich?" But I've created Intellectual Property, and it's just not possible to do that and put in enough time to stay in the high-living lifestyle (unless you've got a trust fund already). But I'm close, and I'm focused on the work, not so much on the money - since the work has to come first. But I'm not far off.

Tuesday, May 10, 2005

Wolf's in Jail, Mama Rose Too

I strolled out into Jackson Square Saturday and there was Dealer Tommy (he sells dope). He said Wolf, the trombone player who's always out playing music in the Square, got put in jail. He had some old warrants or something. Tommy didn't know exactly what for, but it couldn't have been much more than Drunk in Public. And Mama Rose, who I couldn't really place, was in there too.

Sooner or later, just about everyone out there takes a turn at OPP, to make their requisite contribution to the prison-industrial complex here in the State of Incarceration - the highest rate of incarceration of anywhere in the world - that's right, more than Iraq, China, Libya, and all those bad places. It wouldn't be so bad if it actually worked, but crime here is still rampant, people aren't safe anywhere, so it's not really about crime, it's about money. And the 'Haves' are rarely, rarely adversely affected by the systematic fraud that is called justice here. It's just a rape of the underclass. Modern slavery.

From Bacon to Bestiality, The Judge & Cheesepot Toast

Oh, my, what a night!

Friday was the patron dinner benefit at Antoine's. Since they're doing a Black & White Ball in a week and a half, they wanted to feature a Truman

199

Capote character, so I took two scenes from my play that featured Truman Capote and edited them. They had a 'Truman' but I scrambled all week and couldn't find any actors to play Brando or Gore Vidal or Tennessee so I re-wrote the final scene and cut Tenn out and played (read) Brando myself in the first scene, and quickly put on a sport coat and hat and played Gore Vidal in the next. We only did one read-through the night before, so it was a little dicey. It came off pretty well and really was a lot of fun! I had some trepidations, but I convinced myself that this would be as good of a place as any to do an acting debut, and that if I couldn't stand behind my words, then I'd never make it as a playwright. Besides, I can do that stuff, I'm not some introverted recluse playwright. Usually.

So I had fun with it, changing out of my tux and into a white tank top (or "wife beater" shirt, as Christine said) to play Brando in front of the formally-dressed crowd. Larry S., who we discovered grew up in Clinton, Iowa, 30 miles from where I grew up, played Truman - and he did it well. He even looks the part too. Actually, in the 1970s he met Truman at Studio 54 and Truman flew him and a friend to London and he spent a weekend docked on Truman's yacht - and John Lennon was there too. Anyway, it was great to hear the crowd laugh! One line though, just sat there, and no one laughed - and I was appalled! I felt like saying, "HEY! That was <u>funny</u> – you fucks!" Of course, they also laughed in a couple of places that I didn't think they would. Overall, it was really a validating experience.

Sitting at our table, the premier table, was a judge, a younger, 40ish guy, we'll call him Judge X., from across the lake. He's a huge guy, with a quick wit and an appetite for life. The table conversation went from bacon to bestiality! He told some good stories from his experiences on the bench, like the guy accused of crimes against nature, who didn't flinch when Judge X. explained to him that bestiality was having sex with cows, goats, pigs - even chickens - which finally shocked the guy. "Chickens!?" Like he would draw the line THERE. It was funny as hell. I told the story that Brando used to about fucking ducks in stocks at Le Canard Bleu outside of Paris after WWII. Up your cloaka! As dinner progressed, we ended up talking about weed and Judge X.'s wife - well, I found out later that it was actually his girlfriend - (I was the last one at the table to know - and no one else seemed to mind) talked about how high you get when you melt the pot into cheese and spread it on toast. Then, the Judge was laughing about a guy who used to say he got such good pot, that it was, "gov'ment shit." Like the government grows the best weed. He said it with such a drawl it was funny. After champagne and many glasses of wine, we retired to Gennifer Flowers' club across the street. Her husband Finis was there, but she wasn't. I like Finis. Then we went to the Chart Room. I slammed beers, celebrating another rung on the theatrical ladder. Judge X.'s girlfriend and Christine were on each of my biceps, squeezing them and getting all juiced up. Maybe it was the wife beater shirt earlier that gave them a taste? On all subjects Judge X. and I clicked pretty good, as perhaps we're intellectual equals, and he doesn't get much of that. Also, he does acting, and I think he liked my scenes. He said it was good dialogue and that maybe we could meet and go over something he's been working on. He also instructed me on a few legal points. So that was a great, fun night.

Thursday, May 12, 2005

Ups & Downs, Ups & Downs

Well, let's see - looks like I've cured my addiction for blogging - it's been a whole two days now.

It started with putting on my newly-mended seersucker blue shorts and stashing a few hundred dollars in my lockbox at home and heading out for a cold can of PBR at the Tiki Bar on Decatur in the afternoon. Just needed to chill.

The place was full of mostly stinky and disheveled gutter punks - they live on about the same budget and schedule as me apparently - but I took a spot at the end of the bar and pretended to watch the afternoon movie they had on, but I was mostly interested in my cold $1.75 beer.

I just had that one, then figured I needed to get going to somewhere else with a little better karma. I was about five blocks up the street when I realized that my wallet was gone! My heart dropped down my throat. Someone had bumped into me, while I was deep in thought, so I first thought I'd been pick pocketed. If so, I figured it was gone. But if not, there was a rapidly-decreasing chance it was at the bar - so I sprinted back down the street and into the bar. "Oh you're back," the bartender said, as if nothing was amiss. Well, she handed me my wallet and I was so so relieved! I offered the guy who had found it a drink, which he refused, saying it was a matter of honesty (an honest gutter punk!) and so I bought the bartender a drink and tipped her five bucks. I was SOoooooooooooooooo grateful to get it back.

So, of course, I had to go out and celebrate a little bit!

Had some fun and ended up talking a little while with Rosecart Bobby and No Legs James. Had a good time. Bobby said that feeling of having your wallet missing from your pocket is "the worst feeling in the world" and he was right!

Thursday, May 19, 2005

Cheese Steaks, Near Scrapes & Good Pussy

Just returned Wednesday night from the big annual trade association conference and expo in Philly. It went pretty well.

I spoke with Nick Rhodes in L.A., a great friend of mine who I met in college. Nick and I have perfect confidence in each other, I gave him some business advice and helped support him morally on his way up, and he's always there for me. I think he's probably the only one who really 100% believes I can pull off what I can pull off. He has vision. Most people don't.

G.K. was supposed to call me when she got off work and got paid and loan me a hundred bucks or so for cabs and food. I've helped her out in a pinch. But she never called, and she never showed. I waited up until almost 3 AM for her, and I had to get up at 4:30AM. She's like that, though, I bring her breakfast in bed, and she blows me off. I buy her a cute little summer outfit, and she throws it in the corner, refusing to wear it. She's worn my patience now. Stupid bitch. I loan her money in a pinch, and then a month or two later she's in trouble because she loaned out money to a relative (again). Anyway, she's got some PERFECT always-erect nipples and she's a lot of fun to drink with.

So I made it to Philly, then got in touch with Sexy T. We'd been talking on the phone for six months or so.

So Sexy T. came over to the hotel bar and we had martinis and cosmos at the bar until we were sufficiently giddy and we proceeded to the room for a romp. A very nice romp indeed. She's got a pretty face, a nice smile, and huge, bouncy breasts with sensitive nipples. I licked them with delight.

A few nights later, Sexy T. called and said she wanted to come pick up the

VIP museum pass she'd loaned me. Problem was, I was talking to B.K. and she wasn't feeling so hot but by the end of the conversation she said she'd take a shower and come over. I told her I was going down to the bar, and that I'd call for messages and call her back. Well, I sat at the bar again with Sexy T., and we did martinis and cosmos until we were sufficiently giddy and we proceeded to the room for a romp. A very nice romp indeed. Again. Only this time, she did a few more horny things and she had this massive orgasm while I was fucking her with her legs pinned back and hoisted over my shoulder. She's a screamer. And all the while, the phone rang intermittently, since B.K. had taken it upon herself to arrive, virtually unannounced. Apparently she had a nice, low-cut blouse and a short skirt, and she'd trimmed her landing strip (only one reason I can think of for that!) but some guys from a company at the expo ended up telling her how I was missing out and that if I'd seen her I wouldn't have stood her up. She even had the bartender check to see if I was there and she found out I closed my tab two hours earlier. Well, shit. I didn't think she was coming, since she didn't feel too well, and I thought that she surely wouldn't some if she hadn't talked with me to confirm it.

So if I'd played it right I probably could've nailed both of them, but I went for the bush in the hand, rather than the two birds in the tree.

Sexy T. and I went to what I think was Steve's on South Street for real cheese steak. It was good, but nothing like the mouth-melting flavors you get in New Orleans.

I returned home to a clean apartment - I made a deal with Patty to clean up the place, and I let her and her boyfriend stay here and even eat some of my food, since they are really homeless, and a hotel room costs about $30 a night. I wasn't crazy that they'd eaten half my frozen chicken and some other stuff, but I suppose I'll get through it. I thought that they could get back on their feet with this little break, but I saw them during my morning walk Thursday and they were saying how broke they were again. That was disappointing. I guess they probably just lived it up (if you can call it that) a little and since the stress of homelessness is HUGE, they just drank up that little respite.

Thursday, May 26, 2005

Jackson Squared, My Novel

Just to break things up a bit, I thought I'd put a little of my novel out there. I've been thinking a lot about it lately, that I have to put the final touches on it and move forward, since nothing's really happening with this agent who is looking at it. Remember, this is FICTION!

JACKSON SQUARED

A Novel

By

Robert Smallwood

CHAPTER ONE

The train ride through the mountains and then the boundless plains proved a good tonic for my troubles. It gave me time to reflect on a mostly good business career and marriage and to look forward to my new true and artful life, which I did with a bottle of crisp wine or cold beer at lunch and sometimes a martini before dinner.

Maybe I was making up for lost time but drinking and thinking were about the most comfortable way to pass the miles. I was within myself. The scenery never bored me since many scenes flickered in my head. By the time the City of New Orleans pulled out of view of the snow-spotted

Chicago stockyards I had thoroughly pondered my recent fate and made peace with it – as best I could. Things were together, they seemed to all make sense at night when I went to sleep, but an uneasiness had set in by the time I awoke, things seeming a little off, until I thought on it through the day and answered thorny questions to myself. As the days passed, I was better prepared to begin the new life I daydreamed of. The train approached each station closer to New Orleans – Jackson, Brookhaven, McComb, Hammond – while I gained momentum, and instinct. A new chapter in my life was opening: one as an artist, a non-materialist, a free spirit of sorts who would only be concerned with the day before me and the works I would create. This desire had popped up like a balloon shooting to the water's surface, not to be submerged again. Like Natives or Spiritualists, or the hippies in the sixties, I now had No Appointments, No Daily Rush, No Rat Race. The business world was forever away.

Just the canvas the brushes the colors and me.

I arrived in New Orleans with the yearning of a freshman. A double screwdriver made with orange juice that had nearly soured strengthened my resolve but twisted my stomach. I stepped out and wavered on the platform, breathing my first breath of New Orleans air – thick, smarmy, delicious, and rum-soaked. After locking my bag at the station, I walked out into the brightness and fiddled with a map until I pointed myself toward the old section of the city, the French Quarter. I stepped through the stickiness of Bourbon Street past the blaring brass and Zydeco while vomit and spoiled liquids stung my nostrils. Strolling on through Jackson Square, I paused and listened to a lively Dixieland band that seemed to be led by a gentle, extraordinarily large black man playing a dented and weathered old tuba, pausing only to hoist small children on his knee for snapshots. Artists sold their works along the cast iron fence behind.

Deeper into the French Quarter, I was drawn to an intriguing little shop with magic potions, powders, incense, and various other trinkets, supposedly possessing magical powers. Looking over the bizarre collection of mystical books, I squeezed past the wooden figurines and dolls, making my way to the back, where behind a silk curtain sat a matronly fortuneteller with a rosy face and inviting smile. She motioned to me while nodding and rubbing some smooth stones in her palm. I reluctantly agreed to a short sample 'psychic reading' thinking that it couldn't hurt to have the spirits on my side but I had no idea what to expect and probably wouldn't have sat down if it weren't for the effects of the cocktail...

"What do you want to know? Your past or your future?"

"Future, I suppose. I already know the past."

"All right, Doll, let's see what the cards say. Pick ten from the deck. Anywhere. Anywheres in the deck."

"Any ten?"

"Yes, any of them."

She proceeded to finger and examine the cards, snapping them down in a certain pattern, like dominoes. Passing over each one, she offered an interpretation of their meaning and connection to fate while tediously studying my eyes. Time slowed. The room seemed to close in and darken as she progressed.

"And your final card ... oh, Death Card! OutSTANDing!" cried the woman.

"Outstanding? Oh, great. Lost my business and my wife - now I'm dead," I said. *This wasn't going well.*

"Oh, no, no, no. It's a GOOD card. My favorite card, Doll," she said. *I wanted to believe her.*

"A good card? How can death be a *good* thing?"

"It doesn't mean death," she insisted.

"Death is death, isn't it? Dead, done, kaput?"

"No, doll..."

"Then what?"

"Ch… change. A force for change. Change, transition, out with the old, in with the new. That's all."

"Yeah, death would be a change."

"Oh, don't worry Doll. Change is usually or eventually good."

Saturday, May 28, 2005

Algiers Point and The Perfect Day

The day before yesterday was as close to perfect as a day can be in New Orleans, or almost anywhere. It was the ideal blend of spontaneity and familiarity. It was so good that I just savored it yesterday - I couldn't write about it. It was a day I hope I won't ever forget, one that I want to relive when I'm old and infirmed and weakly smiling at a small collection of loved ones on my deathbed. It was absolutely wonderful. And SO New Orleans.

It was a Thursday, not quite the weekend, but the long weekend approaching made it nearly a Friday, and I'd done what I could do early in the week and capped it with an unusually productive Wednesday. I stepped outside on the balcony and there was G.K., looking up with her cute little brown face split with a smile asking, "Are you ignoring me?"

The buzzer on my door hadn't been working well since my son had disabled it one day by bending back the old-fashioned metal ringer so he could happily continue what he was doing without having to hear me ringing to let me in. He has a funny habit of locking me out, which gives him immeasurable pleasure, even though he is 16 and not 6.

So I let G.K. in and she came up, her skin moist from the walk in the warming late spring. "You wanna go for breakfast?" she asked. This surprised me, in fact, it surprised me that she was there at all, since a couple of nights before she was trying to convince me that working as a cocktail server at a strip club on Bourbon was her only option to pay her bills this summer, since the swanky hotel job was already slacking up on hours. I guess she spent the night partying at the club, the nicest one on Bourbon, but smarmy nevertheless. She sat with the manager and found out what a fast and loose and whorish atmosphere it is, and decided that maybe I was right, and she could just somehow struggle through it. After all, with her current credentials, she could land any service job in the city.

So we skipped on down into the French Market and stopped at the quaint, naturally light Cafe de Mello - my second time in a week and ever - and we had a nice breakfast of eggs and grits. We'd gotten to the point where we could be candid about other people's looks and sexuality, so when a pretty girl with blossomy hips bounded toward us through the window, I pointed her out - and just then a huge FedX truck pulled up and completely blocked my view! We just broke out laughing and I never saw that girl again! But she had some hips, and G.K. doesn't really, so I said jokingly, "Yeah, but she doesn't have as nice of titties as you-" and just then I noticed our waitress was pouring me an extra cup, and clearly overheard. So snickering, laughing, I apologized to her and she replied, "Oh, don't worry, my husband's right over there. I hear that stuff all the time." She and G.K. exchanged knowing looks and smiles.

By now G.K. was just about on the floor. We giggled and laughed our way through the newspaper sections we'd picked up from the counter, read our horoscopes and then made our way out and between the crafts and dresses and hats of the vendors' carts.

"What do you want to do?"

By now, any thoughts of going back to my computer to work had been exorcised.

"Let's go to Algiers Point. I've wanted to take the ferry over there for a while. It's free."

"Alright. What do you want to do over there?"

"Just walk around the neighborhood. Maybe go find the Old Point Bar."

"OK."

It was getting to be about noonish and we headed down along the river to the landing, and didn't have to wait more than five minutes for the ferry. We climbed on, up and down stairs like school kids, and marveled at the swiftness of the crossing, and the fact that anyone can get these heavy iron boats to float.

Once there, we ambled through the cobblestone streets, peering at the bars, snowball stands and quaint little gingerbread houses. It was so quiet, so peaceful. We spoke to a white-haired old man who was selling his house, who told us about the houses there.

"All of them from the big house down there on down were built in 1896 - 'cause there was a fire that burned them all down, 'cept that one, it was built in 1905, 'cause it was the stables 'fore that," he said, smiling. He was selling his for $347,000, and he'd bought for $18,000, thirty years ago. He was just so pleasant and trusting, it was wonderful.

What a nice place.

Then we shuffled further down the sidewalk, pointing out the uniqueness of the houses and gardens in the front yards, until we asked a woman where the Old Point Bar was. She was nice too, as nice as could be, she pointed us toward it, and we continued on.

You'd hardly know that some pretty and promising teenage Asian girl had been cut down with a bullet to the face while working at her family store nearby the week before.

We were along the levee now, and down one street divided by a little park sat a little girl, as content as only a little girl can be, perched on the curb with a kitten nearby. Her mother was across the street, keeping a watchful eye while she swept the driveway. It was a perfect picture. A sort of Norman Rockwell New Orleans scene.

We rang the buzzer at the Old Point Bar, and the young woman let us in. It was classic New Orleans, wooden and airy, smelling sugary and lived-in. I ordered a Dixie, as the day called for it, and G.K., who had been lamenting about her being financially short and not able to afford her annual trip to Jamaica with a group of friends, ordered a Red Stripe. The beers were cold and almost immediately perspiring. The bartender - it was just the three of us there - slipped over to take a try at the video poker machine, while I further marveled at the history of the place. After half the beer was gone, I had the occasion to study the slats of cypress on the bathroom walls, as I rather uneasily excreted the previous day's ingestions.

That beer lasted for what seemed like hours, and we ambled out back into the sunlight and humidity, and weaved our way through the neighborhoods on what was becoming the Perfect Day.

We took the ferry back. It was even faster at crossing this time and we got a water's-edge view from the lower deck while saying a wistful goodbye to peaceful Algiers Point. No wonder William S. Burroughs liked shooting smack and writing over there. So serene.

In the apartment to cool off, I fought to decide what to do next. My son was at the computer, I was low on cash, we were most of the way through the Perfect Day, so what to do?

Then it came to me: I had paid up my credit at Brennan's restaurant on Royal, so we could eat a lavish meal and pay for it later - much later. I dressed up a little, and changed from sandals to loafers. Would they let her in in jeans? Sure, there are always a lot of tourists there. So we headed out.

The streets were filling with wine snobs arriving for the Memorial Day Food & Wine Experience celebration, which they have every year mostly on Royal Street. We slipped in to the pink building famous for Bananas Foster and crept over to the bar. I ordered a mojito and she ordered a vodka and soda. When the bill came, I quickly said, "It's a house account."

"Last name, sir?"

I told him, wondering if there would soon be a great social embarrassment attributed to my name in front of the group of spoiled, Uptown, seersucker-clad, old-money types that had gathered for drinks. Like that spoiled-ass writer Michael Lewis. Even the good and proper city council woman was there.

The bartender was taking some time. I took a big gulp of my drink so if it was getting taken away, at least I'd have gotten that.

"Do you need the number?" I asked.

No, no, he had it, he said.

Well, he acted as if everything was fine so we sat down and looked out into the garden patio where a private party was starting, and sipped our drinks.

I decided we were ready for the big hit, so I went to the front and asked for a table for dinner. They seated us faster than I wanted to. I'd expected to get another drink in on the tab. But I signed that one - it was twenty-two bucks just for those two drinks so what the hell. What - was this the fucking Waldorf?

Mouth-watering escargot in garlic butter, then the royal appetizer, Oysters Rockefeller, followed by a delicious spinach salad and between it all I sipped on a martini and a couple of beers. She loosened up and ordered a glass of wine. This was fabulous. We laughed and giggled - I think she even snorted a laugh once accidentally which made us laugh even more. The idea that I was flat busted and we were here living it up was just hilarious. "If these people only knew!" But I would pay it all - eventually.

Our waiter was some very smart, tall, dark, handsome exotic mix of a young man, like Arabic and East Indian, spoke three languages and was studying linguistics and going for his masters. Very impressive.

They brought the grilled redfish with lump crabmeat and three shrimp - (er, "shwimps" here) which was just wonderful. The Perfect Day was continued with a Perfect Meal. We topped it off with two cups of that strong chicory coffee and a snifter of Drambuie. Ahh! She ordered a cheesecake to go and we went. It was going to be maybe two hundred fifty bucks, but man, it was great. And I'd be back in the chips soon enough, right?

We circled the Quarter for a while and ended up by the river front with a bottle of vodka and some juice. It wasn't the best, after a nice big meal like that, but watching the ships and ferry on the river just one more time, and especially at night, was worth it.

We went back home, too tired and full to even get past the thought of further carnal indulgences.

We drifted off to sleep in my little bed, into a peaceful memory of the Perfect Day.

Monday, May 30, 2005

Hunter S. Thompson and Putting Some Sun in a Rainy Day

The day started slowly, I called G.K. and she actually picked up the phone, and said she'd be over after she "washed her hair." I know that those are code words for "three or four hours."

So I called Greg, my best friend since I was 6, back in Iowa, mostly to talk about getting my teenager in line, since his mother had had it with him, and Greg's kid is the same age. We talked for about an hour and Greg told me a funny story about getting on TV at a Cubs game - but good thing he had cleared it with his boss.

219

That boy of mine needs a boot camp or something. That boy is LAZY! But I was in much more trouble when I was his age, stealing my brother's Thai stick and smoking it while drinking lime vodka with Kip; screeching to a halt after plowing over a stop sign at the bottom of the 18th Street hill by Duck Creek; and, of course, banging any fresh Iowa high school beaver I could get a hold of (which was pretty scarce!).

Having not really settled anything, but enjoying the conversation with Greg, I went out to Jackson Square and mingled a bit. Terry the hat lady (with the great toothy smile) was busy weaving hats and selling them from her cart and she mentioned that Codrescu and Doug Brinkley were doing a tribute to Hunter S. Thompson that night. It intrigued me. I think she was sort of hinting at wanting to go but cute little G.K. was already in transit.

G.K. showed up and we went to The Abbey Bar, and they had burgers on the grill and baked beans and all, so I headed straight back to eat, being absolutely starving.

I ate greedily outside under the canopy while the rain sprinkled down, and G.K. continued a lament of her imagined woes. We went back inside and I ordered a Dixie and a water and asked Gracie, if it wasn't too much trouble, could I pay her next week? She said, "I've got a comp account," and she rang them up and gave them to me for free.

Great! Being a regular has its advantages.

Like last night, when I asked Bear at Coop's if I could pay for the beers on Wednesday, that I was a little tight, and he said, "How tight?"

"Really tight."

"OK. No problem. Just come in Wednesday."

Great.

So back to the Abbey, G.K. decided, even though she isn't a meat eater, (boy do I know that!!) that she'd have half a burger and some beans anyway. So I went back to the courtyard and fixed her a plate.

Of course, then we walked home and she was too stuffed to do much of anything, so she laid down on the couch and I wrapped her up in a blanket and pulled out the loveseat bed and we both took a nice nap. I needed it anyway.

I got up and made some coffee and as I was sitting on the balcony sipping and coming to, she started to stir inside. I had looked in the *Times-Picayune* and the Hunter Thompson thing was starting at 7 PM, which meant 8 or so New Orleans time, and it was getting past 7:30. So I poured G.K. a cup of coffee - black, since the creamer from Cafe de Mello had run out - and we sat contently on the balcony chatting. She agreed it might be an interesting thing so we got it together and went over to the Goldmine for the reading.

We got there right in the middle of it, the good part, I suppose, and Doug Brinkley was blasting out facts and stories about Thompson, like the scholarly brain that he is. Codrescu got up and profusely thanked Brinkley, who had profusely lauded Codrescu in his introduction. Then Andrei read a little bit from, *Fear & Loathing in Las Vegas,* and then made a few comments about the two meetings he'd had, and how he could hardly understand a word Thompson was mumbling at Lucky's Bar on St. Charles the month before he blew his brains out. He also said that Amy Carter was there and Codrescu made the skin between her freckles turn pink by telling her he thought her mother was sexy.

Then there were some questions from the audience, and Brinkley told of how HST had had a hip and knee replaced, and that suicide was always an option for him. He was somewhat obsessed with Hemingway in that vein, and always swore he never wanted to be old and infirm. But having arrived at 60, he had become, "the new OLD." He'd lost some good friends, like George Plimpton (I fetched one of Plimpton's last Cokes at last year's Tennessee Williams Literary Festival) and others in the last year and he never thought he'd outlive many of his peers.

I sort of liked HST's all-out "gonzo" style, but I swear, I picked the wrong book to read. I bought, *Fear & Loathing in America* when it came out and it was so grueling and boring, really, that I feared and loathed reading it. It was just a bunch of repetitive letters, mostly. Some of it was real good, but I'm sure I should've read some more of his earlier stuff.

Andrei said that HST's big contribution was really getting to the truth, and then he gave examples of how today's short attention span media routinely cuts out the truth. He seemed to be genuinely lobbying the younger writers to reach deeper, and get at the truth.

OK, let me try that.

I got a chance to talk to both Doug and Andrei briefly, and Codrescu even hugged me after he hugged Brinkley, which is a pretty rare thing for him, I think, being the rough and insolent Eastern European he is. But it was cool. I had to let them both know about the upcoming meeting for the New Orleans Writers Museum and that the Governor had signed a proclamation declaring September, "Writers Appreciation Month," and that was going to be our launching pad. I told Doug I wanted to do a "Festival of Books," sort of thing by the river with poetry and plays and all and I'd need his help.

So we left and walked over to the A&P to get a couple of beers, which took G.K. probably 15 minutes to fucking decide what she wanted. But the cooler always feels good in the A&P when summer approaches and the humidity starts up again.

Still longing for Jamaica, G.K. ended up with a Red Stripe. Of course, I had
to open it on a fire hydrant, causing myself a minor injury since it wasn't a
twist-off.

I was starving again, I mean, it was getting near 10 PM, and so we went into
the Bourbon House, another of Dickie Brennan's places. I just wanted a
po-boy (the New Orleans term for a "sub" or "hoagie") or something
equally appetizing. And, I tried out my credit there yesterday and it went
beautifully.   How many new restaurants can the Brennans open up?
Anyway, the Oysters Bienville and spinach salad and my credit were good,
and so I was back. G.K. was just laughing that I was trying to pull off
another (seemingly) larcenous meal.

But the bar was full and I saw the bartender from yesterday and got sort of
a bad, suspicious vibe so I decided we'd go to the Palace Café around the
corner - another of Dickie's places. Sterling choice.

We had some of that fantastic crabmeat cheesecake, and a shrimp
remoulade. Now I was drinking Heineken and she was sipping a Long
Island Tea.

Then we ordered a bleu cheese and romaine lettuce salad, and some veggie
plate, which turned out to be a tasteless portabella mushroom with bad
cheese on top. So I sent it back and replaced it with the pan roasted oysters

and things were grand. I had another beer, she had a glass of wine and I topped it off with a wet Absolut martini, straight up, with olives (my usual).

We had a wonderful conversation with the bartender, and G.K. was finally convinced that working for the swanky hotel just wasn't like working with a local, family-owned business at all. And she needed at least a second job now - if she was going to "make rent" and ultimately Jamaica.

We strolled back to my little place on Madison, and I put a pot of decaf on and we sipped coffee and watched the rain come down lightly.

The only time the Quarter is ever really fresh is after a good rain.

"It's going to be a good morning tomorrow," I said.

We clowned around a little bit with my digital camera, but I never got a good pic of her. She wasn't looking too girly anyway, with a baseball cap on and jeans - but she took one of me that was actually pretty good. Laughing, of course.

Other than that, I have got so much going on, that I hardly know where to start. At least I got this blog out tonight, while the memory is still fresh. But I do have real work to do this week, computer consulting stuff, so I can make some fucking money and pull out of this terrible spin :)

Tuesday, May 31, 2005

"Not for Me"

Well, I tried and tried everything to get rolling today, but I had a foggy feeling in my head and a sense of uneasiness in my stomach. Also, there are the usual aches and pains from working out, but now I have them from not working out. I drank coffee, did some yoga, ate, took a walk along the river, jerked off, had a smoke, tried to nap, took a shower and still nothing could shake these doldrums. And I was SO looking forward to getting out of the gate today and making it a good ending to the month and a good beginning of the rest of my life.

So I just forced myself to make a couple of sales-related phone calls, but thank God, they weren't in, so I could just leave a little "touching base" voice mail and putter around some more. If I had aspirin I'd take it.

What happened? My horoscope said I'd have a spring in my step today. I tried to believe it. But the day's not over, right?

Oh, and that lazy arrogant bitch of an agent Uptown, Pam A., who has sat on my novel for nearly four months now, said that (even after two years of re-working it), "It's not for me."

The Five People You Meet in Hell: Surviving Katrina

The words of death in the book business.

"Too much travelogue, not enough story." Well, that's the point, stupid cunt. And that's what she said last time. I'll bet she didn't even read it again. Arrogant bitch. I want people to have fun reading it, and mostly people who don't live here. Well, she doesn't even like the most famous book ever written here, *Confederacy of Dunces*, the Pulitzer-prize winner by John Kennedy Toole. Probably too much travelogue for her. I told her about Brinkley and Codrescu's tribute to Hunter Thompson and she replied, "I don't like Codrescu."

She probably doesn't like edgy stuff like drinking or fucking either.

I didn't think so. Too busy reading absurd romance novels and cramming that rubbery dildo up your dry hole.

Well, good. Now I can move on, unfettered by the small minds of the established publishing world (see quotes by Einstein, etc.). What the fuck do they know anyway? Their business is dying because they've had their heads in the sand. What really new things have they done? Any innovations in content? Nope. Any innovations in publishing format? Nope. Structure? Nope. Marketing? Nope. Oh wait, there's Harry Potter. So this Uptown spoilt bitch has a couple of authors and she can mooch off of them without anyone really ever getting anywhere.

Can't believe I wasted almost three fucking years thinking that that stupid bitch could be the one to team up with just because she's the only agent in town. Fucking worthless. So off I go into the wild blue and the possibilities are endless. I think I need a wet Absolut martini or two, so I can think this stuff out.

Henry and My Play

I decided to work on my play a little this morning. I canceled out of going to a meeting in Baton Rouge - so I have a day to catch up. I'd rather work on my play than almost anything, and not having it fixed right bothers me.

Henry Hood was a friend of mine who died in December. He was 72. An "old" 72. I met him a couple of years ago and became interested in his stories about Tennessee Williams, Brando and others. It all checked out, too. So I'd bring him a bottle, clean his apartment, give him a bath and listen to his stories.

Here's the beginning of my (re-written) play. It gets better, but here's a little of it:

BRANDO, TENNESSEE & ME

An original play in two acts

April, 2005

This play is dedicated to Henry Hood

The persons of the play

- HENRY
- KID
- MARLON BRANDO
- TRUMAN CAPOTE
- TENNESSEE WILLIAMS
- GORE VIDAL
- NORMAN MAILER
- BARTENDER (2)

ACT I

Characters: BRANDO should be a look-alike from age 20-30 who can imitate Brando's early acting style. TENNESSEE & TRUMAN should also be as close in looks and mannerisms as the real characters were themselves, and may be played by the same actor, separated by the two acts. MAILER is a robust, smaller man, with protruding ears. BARTENDER in Act 1 and GORE are the same actor, Bartender (frumpy, not-very-convincing drag queen) in Act 2 and MAILER are the same actor.

Scene: Henry is sprawled out, passed out drunk in front of the Abbey Bar in the French Quarter. Several scenes from the 1940s and 1950s periodically play out as Henry reflects on his memories.

Time: *Early 21ˢᵗ century*; Place: *French Quarter, New Orleans.*

Although vivid, this is a memory play. The first scene takes place outside of the Abbey Bar in the French Quarter. He is carrying on a conversation with KID, the young inquisitor, (who is actually Henry as a young man). A popular old Southern song, "Are You from Dixie? ('Cause I'm from Dixie Too)" is playing on the piano. Henry lays disheveled and drunk against the exterior wall of The Abbey. Kid strolls up and starts to shake him awake.

KID: Sir? Hey, you! You OK? Hey mister, you OK? Wake up. You gotta get up. Hey! YOU OK?

HENRY: *(Gradually waking.)* Huh? Uh? Wha-?

KID: Are you OK, mister? Come on, let's get you up.

HENRY: Wha-? Where? What time is it?

KID: It's past three a.m. You gotta get up. They'll arrest you. C'mon, sir.

HENRY: Huh? Who are you, kid?

KID: Nobody. Just passing by. You need to get up and get yourself together.

HENRY: Where's my Lily? *(say, 'li-lee')*

KID: I don't know. You were out here passed out by yourself.

HENRY: Oh...

KID: You OK?

HENRY: Yes, yes, I'm all right.

KID: Good. Get yourself up, c'mon.

HENRY: Easy, Kid. My hip! I broke it a while back.

KID: Sorry.

HENRY: These damn sidewalks in the Quarter.

KID: OK. Let's get you home. Where do you live?

HENRY: We live upstairs from Miss Dixie.

KID: Where?

HENRY: Over on Bourbon Street, across from Lafitte's. Where my Lily plays nightly.

KID: OK, let's get you home. Can you walk OK?

HENRY: Yes, yes, I can walk. Just a little limp. Hey, let's go in - get an eye-opener.

KID: No, no. I think you've had enough.

HENRY: Do you have two dollars you could lend me, Kid?

KID: C'mon-

HENRY: I'll repay you tomorrow.

KID: I'm gonna make sure you get home.

HENRY: Oh, alright then.

The two walk off into the darkness of center stage, after pausing in the darkness, they arrive at Lafitte's Blacksmith Shop bar.

HENRY: Alrighty. This is close enough. Thanks, Kid.

KID: You sure?

HENRY: Yes, this is fine. Hey Kid, I hate having to ask you, but could you loan me that two dollars? I get paid tomorrow.

KID: I don't think I should. You need to go home.

HENRY: Well then how about buying me a drink? I can buy you one tomorrow. I'm just out of cash, Kid.

KID: Um-

HENRY: Let's go in for a nightcap, what do you say?

KID: That's probably not a good idea, mister.

HENRY: Hey, I was somebody. I've got some stories for you. I've had quite a life. Do you know who I am, young man?

KID: Uh, no-

HENRY: I'm Henry Hood, Jr. My great-grandfather was General Hood – from the Civil War. You know Fort Hood? That's on my father's side.

KID: OK.

HENRY: And I'm a Barrymore on my mother's side – yes, yes, that's right, that sassy Drew – and I was an actor in New York, Rome. Even a director! I knew some V-E-R-Y famous people, like Marlon Brando, Tennessee Williams, the playwright – and other famous writers too.

A light softly shines STAGE LEFT on MARLON BRANDO as a young man, who is standing on a black (unseen) pedestal in the dark, so it appears that he is suspended in mid-air, to represent the image in Henry's mind. Then light shines on TENNESSEE and they play out a very short, muted scene while Henry and Kid talk, then the light fades away.

Music softens and then stops.

Thursday, June 02, 2005

Wild Wide Open & Harry Anderson's Opening Night

Wow! Had a couple of days of wild abandon. Yes, it started with those wet martinis, which turned into a raucous night with little G.K. (which was somewhat embarrassing when she replayed the later hours to me the next day).

She skipped off to go hunt for a second job, and I tried to rest and recover, since opening night at Harry Anderson's new place was that night (June 1). It's a new bar with a stage and seating for Harry to do his comic magician act. I was wiped out from the previous night - and a hectic couple of months, but how many opening nights are there?

I showed up around 8:30 for the 9 PM show. You walk in the place down a narrow entrance into a brick courtyard. The bar is tucked in among the bricks like a real speakeasy. People do that here. It reminded me of the great Mardi Gras party after the Krewe du Vieux parade with Walter "Wolfman" Washington's band at a house in the Marigny. Fun as hell. And a little illicit. It was a full moon, I think, and it seemed that it was the best place to be in the universe at that exact time.

Harry's bar is a masculine place, with exposed beams and the original wood floor around the bar. The back of the bar is copper-colored tin that's been distressed. They even retrieved the brass bar foot stand pole from the attic which was at the old Matador Bar, housed there just prior to Harry getting the place. This thing took him an extra year to get off the ground, with all the Vieux Carre Commission red tape and cost overruns. Harry's pretty wife Elizabeth stood sipping Stoli martinis in a black dress. We talked about how they'd re-done the place but left as much of the original wood and bricks as possible. Then it was time to talk with the bartender.

"What kind of beer do you have?"

"We have Maudite, Anchor Steam, PBR..."

"What's the first one?"

"Maudite. It's French-Canadian."

"How do you say it?"

"Maw-deet. I'll buy you the first one, since I know you'll buy the second."

"OK. Cool."

"Here, sir."

"Can I just have it in the bottle?"

"Actually, the way it's brewed, there's sediment in the bottom, so it's better to drink it out of a glass."

"OK. Cool."

The bartender poured a glass that ended up three-quarters full of foam. It was strong but a little sweet. Sort of like Abita Amber, but with more bite and sweetness.

Elizabeth said that they don't carry Bud or Miller products, since they wanted it to be a unique feel - and it really does work. But they do have PBR for the working man.

"Those companies can be totalitarian."

"Yes. Yes they can. I mean, if someone really has to have a Bud, we'll run across the street and buy one at Checkpoint's for them."

"Uh, huh."

There weren't too many people at the bar. I didn't realize that everyone was in the other room and I was lucky to get a seat. There was a table in the back corner and I wanted to see the entire scene. Cameron and his wife from the Abbey were there. She was a little drunk - I'd never seen her tipsy like that. But she was really having fun. Sidney Smith was there – Kalila's ex. Kalila-the-Horror-Filmmaker-and-ghost-tour-guide-pagan-practictioner.

My cell rang just before Harry started, and it was G.K. saying she was heading over.

She showed up 15 minutes later, peering her cute face through the doorway and noticing my waving hand.

Well the Maudite's were going down good and Harry started his show with a (literally) big card trick. He was funny as hell, as usual, with lots of little jokes thrown in during his routines.

"I'm Harry. Well, after all, we all are, aren't we?" (A few chuckles).

"Like my suit? Yeah. It was a surprise present from my wife. It was hanging over the chair when I came home." (Cackles of laughter).

"It even had a wallet in it," he deadpanned, to even louder laughter.

He told about the history of sideshows and freaks, and even did a bit as Elephant Man with a ventriloquist dummy.

It was a good hour of laughter. Hilarious. He did some really funny physical comedy with audience, "volunteers." I chatted with a lady from southern California who I shared our table with. She and her husband had moved here for the summer, and trying to get into the local scene. Well they were in the right place.

Afterward I congratulated Harry and Elizabeth and G.K. and I headed down to Molly's on the Market. We didn't plan it that way, but Harry and Elizabeth showed up a few minutes later. We had a good time, talking with them and a Rastafarian-type African-American male friend of theirs. It was fun, but maybe I got a little too drunk again.

Oh, well. We really really had a good time. And that's worth it.

Then last night I had a crazy dream about someone going up Esplanade Avenue the wrong way, causing a big pile-up wreck, and workmen angrily pulling apart a house they'd just constructed (since they didn't get paid) and Harry having a barbeque at his new place, with little piggies wandering around squealing. What's THAT about??

So today was recovering with carrot juice and going to the grocery and cleaning up. Mostly chillaxing.

Friday, June 03, 2005

"Enough to Feed 900 Niggers in Africa!"

I ate some Grape Nuts and took my little river walk along the levee. Then to the courtyard for crawfish (and beer). They were good, along with the potatoes, garlic and corn, and the Busch Light beers went down like water. Really spicy.

Pillhead Richard, my neighbor, and Pat were there, along with Pillhead's Dad and his wife. Pillhead's Dad told about his recipe.

"You put the crawfish in a tub and purge 'em."

"So they shit first, right?"

"Well, no, actually they just spit. Ya put two things of iodized salt in there and it makes them spit out all that stuff. All the bad stuff. You see that shit line there? That's OK. 'Cause they already done spit all the bad stuff out."

"Yeah?"

"Then ya' soak 'em again in clear water. Then ya' get yer pot and put in yer crab boil and cayenne pepper, lemons, and garlic, celery, mushrooms, onions - everythin' but the potatoes and crawfish. Ya cut the potatoes in half, and ya just put them and the live crawfish in at the same time - for six minutes. Six minutes, exactly. Then ya let 'em soak for 18 minutes."

"Well they sure are good," I said.

"I'm glad you're eatin' yer fill. Ya know what I hate? I hate to see food go to waste. I mean, with the food these restaurants around here throw away, there's enough to feed 900 niggers in Africa. Ha!"

"Dad - uh, don't say that word around here. Come on, let's go down to Sidney's store and give them some of these crawfish. Uh… sorry, man, sometimes my Dad talks too much."

Saturday, June 11, 2005

Bettie at the Beach and George Killed a Man

Bettie and I went to the beach at Waveland today. She and I met 20 years ago or so when she was married and working as a bank teller and I was working my first job. She's cute and petite, and mostly Cajun. We always had this thing for each other but we both were shy and she was married. So we spoke in stilted phrases when I came to her window at the bank. Then one Sunday night at The Dock bar by Lake Pontchartrain I ran into her. I took her hand and she didn't have her ring on. She'd gotten divorced. So within an hour we took a walk on the levee and were soon hiking up her white skirt with her mounting me and fucking away. Some guy walked by, perhaps a local on his nightly walk, and we were still fucking, and we didn't miss a stroke. Then, after a couple minutes he walked back by. We just kept fucking. Then afterward her period came down so I had to go inside and get her sister to retrieve a tampon. She was embarrassed, but I didn't care. I'd just gotten laid, and at 24, that's a top (OK, the ONLY) priority.

Anyway, Bettie picked me up at my place on Madison and we headed out to Bay St. Louis, Mississippi to get some sun at the beach. She said, "I like a beer buzz in the morning," (thanks, Sheryl Crow) so we stopped just before Slidell and got a 12-pack. On the way there, she told me her ex-boyfriend, the wife-beater asshole George, had come home one night after I'd been over there (this was 15 years ago or so) and broke her door down and beat her. We'd just fucked at her Chalmette apartment, but even though they were supposedly broken up, I didn't like the fact that there was no back door, (except hers, which I got into that night!) so I left. Good thing.

Anyway, she told me that he'd killed this black guy – shot him over a drug deal and then taken off for California. He came back to St. Bernard Parish after a few months in exile and nothing ever happened to him.

So if Sheriff Stephens down there in St. Bernard Parish, wants to know, and has the time, George Sc_ _ _ _r killed a man. It's the George Sc_ _ _ _r who's been arrested a bunch: the one who's kid is already in jail for killing someone else. I know you have bigger fish to fry, but call or email me and I'll tell you his name, and how to get in touch with Bettie.

I hope you get him (before he gets me).

Sunday, June 19, 2005

Hanging Out

Hung out at the corner of Royal and Orleans most of the weekend, just talking with Michael and the street artists. There's a new chick on the scene – Iyana. She's a light-skinned woman with really impressive artwork. It's sort of in patterns, I guess she uses a process that creates what she calls, "mono prints," which are basically one-of-a kind prints. She didn't sell any the whole weekend, but I encouraged her by telling her that the more time she puts in the more chance she has of selling. But most of the tourists really want sax players or Louis Armstrong or New Orleans architecture like Michael sells.

We had a real good time, though. Rhonda and the rest of the usual gang were there and we hung out, talked, drank, smoked and enjoyed ourselves. It's a campy little group with a good vibe. Rhonda is funny as hell.

Sunday, June 26, 2005

Hanging Out Some More

Hung out at the corner of Royal and Orleans most of the weekend, again. This time a few more people showed up. There was a girl, probably 20 or so, from Australia. She was here for a job interview but she ended up not liking New Orleans and decided not to stay. She could only see the bad side of the place. Iyana was a little mean and bitchy to her with her comments and jokes, and the Aussie noticed it. Iyana finally sold something, so that's good. A burly black dude came up that I guess Iyana knows and he and the Australian girl went off together, which surprised me, since she didn't seem to trust anyone. Michael and Iyana and Rhonda were smoking a joint in the street and the Aussie asked, "Can you do that here?" And the replies were something like, 'Well, we're doing it, aren't we?"

Also, a guy who works close by dropped in on the conversation, and he noted that, "God was at work here," because of the conversation and camaraderie and vibe. I think he was right. They were precious hours in time. Things are as good as they've ever been here.

I talked for a while with this girl, I think she's about 19, who's a chain-smoking, caffeine-chugging, non-stop talking artist. She told me all about "Burning Man," which is this big gathering of folks celebrating art out in the desert out West. I looked at the website and some people were nude and they had created these huge installation art pieces that were interesting. Apparently, they barter for a lot of stuff and people do a lot of mushrooms, acid, etc. It looks and sounds interesting, but I'm not real sure I would enjoy it at this point in my life. Maybe 20 years ago.

Broderick is a younger African-American guy from north of the lake who has started to hook up with Iyana. She's talking about moving here (again) – she's lived in NYC and Arizona and everywhere – but this summer she's got her kid, who's about 14 or so and lives with his dad in Ohio. Michael said that the other night, before Broderick hooked up with Iyana, he gave her a kiss and she made it into a pretty deep one.

Iyana's good-looking, and Rhonda thinks she's hot too, although Rhonda's girlfriend is a real skinny brunette that works at the art shop on the corner, with the blue Ethyl Kidd Real Estate sign hanging on it.

This is the best summer ever and New Orleans is the best it has ever been. The people are great, the streets are paved, the stoplights work and the movie business is rolling.